CRAFTS
from your
MICROWAVE

CRAFTS
from your
MICROWAVE

**ALISON JENKINS
AND
KATE MORRIS**

NEW
BURLINGTON
BOOKS

A QUINTET BOOK

Published by New Burlington Books
6 Blundell Street
London N7 9BH

ISBN 1-85348-622-1

This book was designed and produced by
Quintet Publishing Limited
6 Blundell Street
London N7 9BH

Creative Director: Richard Dewing
Designer: Nicky Chapman
Senior Editor: Laura Sandelson
Photographer: Nick Bailey

Typeset in Great Britain by
Central Southern Typesetters, Eastbourne
Manufactured in Hong Kong by Regent Publishing Services Limited
Printed in China by Leefung-Asco Printers Limited

DEDICATIONS

To my mother for constant support, and to Pete for
tolerating the mess – Alison

To Bill and Lily – Kate

AUTHORS' ACKNOWLEDGEMENTS

The authors would like to thank Toshiba UK for supplying
the microwave oven used for the photography and in creating
the projects for this book, and The Wild Bunch for help with the
chapter on Dried Flowers.

CONTENTS

INTRODUCTION

~ 1 ~

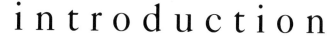

introduction

the versatility of the microwave oven as a food preparation device is now unquestionably established. Defrosting, reheating, baking, and cooking are all simple and quick with a microwave. It has become an essential tool in many kitchens around the world.

For the craft hobbyist, the microwave oven is a machine that can open up a whole realm of new possibilities in creativity, speeding up experimentation with materials as diverse as dyes and dough – as you will see in this volume of colourful and inspirational projects. This book contains over 60 ideas for you to copy or adapt for yourself, using the microwave oven for functions as diverse as dyeing fabric, drying flowers, and papier mâché. There are also some lovely tasty foods to cook and present with flair and creativity.

ABOVE
Microwave ovens have uses far beyond preparing food. Successful craftwork can be achieved in the microwave including dyeing fabric, flowers and papier-mâché.

HOW DOES A MICROWAVE WORK?

Successful craftwork using the microwave oven, just like successful cooking, depends very much on your understanding of how the oven works, so you will need to go back to first principles, and to the instruction book that accompanies your microwave oven.

Microwaves are radio waves of a very high frequency. They are generated by the magnetron, usually sited in the top of the oven, and produce a change in temperature only when they are absorbed into any water and fat molecules within the oven. The microwaves are reflected by metal but pass through glass, pottery, plastics and paper. Both these principles are important to remember, as they affect both the type of craft which can successfully be transferred to the microwave and the type of mould or former which can be used in the processes. The microwaves pass into the food within the oven cavity and cause the water and fat molecules to move very quickly – 2.5 million times a second. This movement causes friction which generates heat. The microwaves penetrate up to 35–50 mm (1–1½ in) deep, so that the centre of any food thicker than 70–100 mm (3–4 in) will be cooked in the conventional method, ie by heat being conducted from the outer areas. To ensure an even spread of the microwaves in the oven (and thus to the food or contents of the oven), a stirrer, fan or turntable, or a combination of these, is incorporated in the design of the oven.

The power of microwave ovens varies from 500 watts to 850 watts depending on the model. The more powerful the oven, the more quickly it will cook. The power level is always adjustable, so that on different settings

LEFT
Hat with tie-dyed sash and roses. There are many fabrics that are suitable for tie-dyeing in the microwave oven.

the oven can be used to defrost, reheat or cook. The number of power levels on an individual oven varies; for maximum versatility five or more power levels are useful, particularly for the hobbyist.

Some microwaves use a clockwork dial for power and timing while others use digital controls with touch-sensitive panels. All incorporate some sort of bell or beep to signal the end of the programmed time. For short cooking times a digital timer will afford far greater control.

Just as with food, many of the craft items shown in this book will benefit from standing time. If you check in the cookery book that came with your oven, you will find that many recipes will detail a standing time. Just as you would remove a sponge cake from the microwave while the edges are still wet and allow the conducted heat to finish off the cooking, so you should err on the gentle side with your craft pieces. Flowers and dough shapes should be removed before they are totally dry to allow the conducted heat to finish off the drying process.

RIGHT
Gingerbread men made in the microwave oven at a fraction of the time they would take to bake in a regular oven.

Because of the way in which the microwaves act on the contents of the oven, the size, density, quantity and shape of the items being cooked can require widely different cooking times – just think of the relatively simple process of baking a potato. This experience needs to be applied at all times to using your microwave for craftwork and will be different for all, depending on the machine, the shapes, the moisture content etc. The rule for craftwork is to err on the gentle side using 50 per cent or 25 per cent power for periods giving you much more room for error – blasting on full power can scorch some areas while others remain moist.

safety rules

*Never leave the oven unattended while in use for a craft project

*Always check items at regular intervals during the cooking/curing process to reduce risk of scorching

*Always check that containers and moulds are microwave safe

*Always read the instruction book for your particular model of microwave and understand the watt rating and different power levels

*Always remove items with great care. Use an oven glove as many items give off steam which can burn and sometimes containers are hot through conducted heat from the item

*Always allow items to stand and cool for five to ten minutes before deciding whether to replace and reheat them in the microwave

Again, referring to the cook book that came with your microwave, you will find instructions on placing foods in the oven. Even if there is a turntable, foods like broccoli which have dense stems need to be carefully positioned for the piece to cook evenly and the rules apply just as much to any craft items you plan to place in the oven. Repositioning during the curing or drying process can make the difference between a successful and an unsuccessful experiment.

COMBINATION MICROWAVE OVENS

If you have a combination microwave oven which offers cooking with both microwaves and fanned warm air, many of the ideas in this book become even easier to recreate. The drying times can be reduced with the fanned warm air helping to remove any moisture from the atmosphere in the oven and thus speeding up the process. Again, you will need to look carefully at the instruction book that came with the oven and carry out your own experiments to assess the ideal cooking times for the individual projects.

LEFT
Drying flowers in the microwave has a dramatic effect on their colours – for example gold turns to bronze and pink turns to lavender.

EXPERIMENTING WITH YOUR MICROWAVE OVEN

Although suggested times are given alongside the projects in this book, the crucial factors of density, humidity, quantity, uniformity and size can greatly affect the cooking or curing time and it is essential that you experiment for yourself. All the times given will err on the safe side and have been calculated on the basis that 700 watts is full power, 350 watts half power and 210 watts 30 per cent power or medium low. Check the instruction book with your own microwave to work out the nearest settings to match these power levels.

containers and moulds

In the midst of creative activity it is easy to forget the golden rules about suitability of different containers for use in the microwave oven. No container with metallic decoration can be used, though wooden containers can. To test whether a container is microwave-safe, put about 200 ml (8 fl oz) of water in a glass measuring jug. Place the measuring jug and the container in the microwave together and cook on high for one minute. The container should still be cool. Remember that some items may be affected by the convected heat from the item around or inside it. Check plastic containers by immersing in very hot water and seeing whether they become more pliable or misshapen.

RIGHT
Materials that are considered microwave-safe are: tempered glass, clay or ceramics, microwave-safe plastic, rubber or cardboard.

SALT
DOUGH

~2~

*b*ased on basic food raw materials, a dough to make shapes and figures has a natural place in the craft kitchen. A highly popular craft material in Scandinavia and the USA, the dough is easy to knead and shape and dries well in the microwave oven so long as you are patient. Once dry, the shapes or figures you have made can be painted and varnished to make permanent decorations for the home.

As your skill develops you will find the dough easier to shape and mould into the required form. By using basic kitchen utensils such as graters, garlic presses, toothpicks, kitchen knives and spatulas you will find that this form of modelling material is a cheap alternative to clay-based commercial products and just as effective. Cake icing suppliers are an excellent source of cutters to make shapes such as flowers and leaves quickly and simply with a variety of sizes to complement your ideas. Simply stick pieces together and smooth out surfaces before drying out the completed piece.

ABOVE
A household grater can be used to model and decorate salt dough.

SAFETY POINTS

The shapes, thicknesses and moisture content of the models will differ so you need to take care when drying them out in the microwave oven. If the surface of the pieces begins to bubble simply switch off and remove from the oven. Level the surface with a spatula, and allow the model to cool before continuing the drying process. Always stay with the oven while the drying cycle is in process in case of scorching – we have assumed that the microwave oven is fitted with a turntable, but you may still have to turn the shapes during the cooking. Remember to rest the pieces at the end of the period of cooking to check their progress as the dough will continue to dry out as it cools on a wire rack.

Make any holes in the dough shapes before you dry them. Holes need to be at least 1 cm (½ in) in from the outer edge if possible to help prevent fracture. Any metal hanging loops, magnets, etc. should be added after the models have been dried and completed, using strong glue.

PAINTING

All the dough projects in the book are based on dried dough shapes decorated with gouache or poster paint, then sprayed or painted with clear

varnish to add gloss. The layer of varnish will also help to stop the dough reabsorbing moisture from the atmosphere, leading to a softening and cracking of your product.

RIGHT
When the item is completely dry it can be painted.

salt dough

1 MIX 1 CUP OF SALT WITH 3 CUPS OF PLAIN FLOUR IN A LARGE BOWL THEN ADD 1 CUP OF COLD WATER. MIX INTO A DOUGH.

3 ROLL OUT THE DOUGH ON A LIGHTLY FLOURED SURFACE TO THE REQUIRED THICKNESS, USUALLY ABOUT 5 MM/¼ IN. SHAPE AND MOULD.

2 TURN THE DOUGH OUT ON TO A LIGHTLY FLOURED SURFACE AND ROLL OR KNEAD UNTIL COMPLETELY SMOOTH. THE DOUGH CAN THEN BE STORED IN A PLASTIC BAG IN THE FRIDGE FOR SEVERAL DAYS.

4 COOK SLOWLY IN THE MICROWAVE, USUALLY ON LOW AND MEDIUM POWER, ALLOWING THE SHAPES TO REST AND COOL ON A COOLING RACK BETWEEN TIMES TO PREVENT OVERCOOKING AND BUBBLING. PAINT AND VARNISH THE DRIED SHAPES TO PRESERVE THE DOUGH.

simple shapes

These chunky dough shapes are ideal for little fingers to play with and robust enough to survive many a tantrum. Big brother or sister can help make them for a younger sibling.

YOU WILL NEED
~

¼ quantity of dough

Cookie cutters or templates

Microwave-safe plate

Cooling rack

Paints

Brushes

Varnish

Medium grade sandpaper

Sharp knife

Rolling pin

Cord

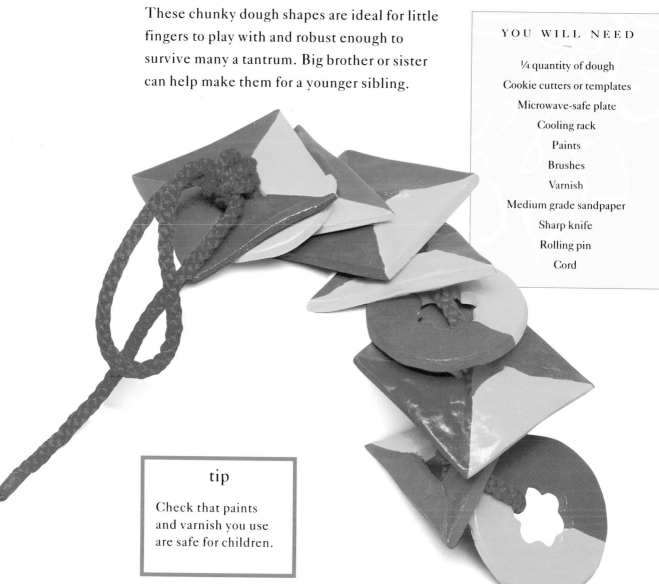

tip

Check that paints and varnish you use are safe for children.

Roll the dough out to 5 mm (¼ in) thickness. Cut out the shapes using the templates on page 104 and transfer on to a microwave-safe plate. Cook on medium low for 10 minutes, check for air bubbles, then cook for a further 3 minutes on medium. Leave to stand on a wire cooling rack. Once the shape is completely cool and dry, sand off any rough edges and paint with primary colours. Finish off with several coats of varnish. String the dough shapes on to a length of brightly coloured cord.

tree trinkets

Make your own cheap decorations for the Christmas tree that will last year after year. Dough is an ideal material for the kids to join in the fun too.

YOU WILL NEED
~

¼ quantity of dough
Cookie cutters or templates
Microwave-safe plate
Cooling rack
Paints and brushes
Varnish
Medium grade sandpaper
Sharp knife
Rolling pin ● Bodkin
Assorted ribbons

Roll the dough out to 5 mm (¼ in) thickness. Cut out the shapes using cookie cutters or the templates on page 104 and make holes with the bodkin in the appropriate position for threading ribbons. Transfer on to a microwave-safe plate and cook on medium low for 10 minutes. Check for air bubbles, then cook for a further 3 minutes on medium. Leave to stand on a wire cooling rack. Once the shapes are completely cool and dry, sand off any rough edges and paint with primary colours. Then varnish. Thread narrow ribbon through the hole in each shape and tie to form a hanging loop. Add a decorative bow to each.

tip

Group matching shapes together to make larger decorations, such as a cluster of stars. Simply repaint the decorations with a different colour if you change your tree colour scheme.

romantic
candlesticks

Laying a romantic table for Valentine's Day or an anniversary need not be expensive if you make your own heart-motif candlesticks like these.

YOU WILL NEED
~

¼ quantity of dough
Rolling pin
Sharp knife
Microwave-safe plate
Cooling rack
Red and white gouache paint
Black permanent marker pen
Brushes • Varnish
Epoxy resin glue
Candles

safety

Never leave the candles burning unattended or allow them to burn down to the candle rings.

Roll out the dough to 5 mm (¼ in) thickness and cut out heart shapes with a sharp knife. Transfer to a microwave-safe plate. Roll out sausage shapes of dough about 1 cm (½ in) diameter with your hands and form into rings to make the supports for the candles – the dough may shrink slightly as it dries so allow for this. Cook all the hearts and candle rings by starting on low for 5 minutes, then 5 minutes on medium low, then 1 to 2 minutes on medium. Check frequently for air bubbles and allow the dough to rest between cooking phases. Leave to cool on a wire rack. Paint all the pieces white, then add a coat of red to the heart shapes. Draw on spots and details with the marker pen before fixing the hearts with glue to the front of the candle rings. Dry thoroughly, then add several coats of varnish.

~PROJECT~

napkin rings

Make every day special with these colourful napkin rings which you can decorate to match your colour scheme.

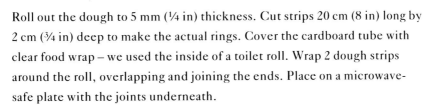

YOU WILL NEED

~

*½ quantity of dough
(makes six napkin rings)*

Rolling pin • Sharp knife

Microwave-safe plate

Bodkin or wooden skewer

Cooling rack

Gouache paint • Brushes

Medium grade sandpaper

Cardboard tube

Clear food wrap

Varnish

tip

You could give the napkin rings a festive touch with red and green paint or, alternatively, spray them gold for special occasions.

Roll out the dough to 5 mm (¼ in) thickness. Cut strips 20 cm (8 in) long by 2 cm (¾ in) deep to make the actual rings. Cover the cardboard tube with clear food wrap – we used the inside of a toilet roll. Wrap 2 dough strips around the roll, overlapping and joining the ends. Place on a microwave-safe plate with the joints underneath.

To make a bow decoration

Cut 2 strips about 2 cm (¾ in) wide by 14 cm (5½ in) long and a strip 1.5 cm (⅝ in) wide by 3 cm (1¼ in) long. Trim the ends of one long strip to make points. Lay the other long strip on top and fold the ends into the centre to make the bow loops. Pinch the centre together then wrap the small strip around to complete the bow.

To make a leaf and flower decoration

Cut a leaf with a sharp knife and mark on the veins. To make a flower, cut a circle about 3 cm (1¼ in) in diameter and cut out 5 small triangles all round leaving 5 petals. Roll a small ball of dough and press into the centre of the flower using a bodkin or wooden skewer.

Complete the 2 napkin rings on the cardboard tube and cook as follows –
5 minutes on low, 5 minutes on medium low, 3 minutes on medium.
Remove the plate from the oven between each phase to allow the shapes to cool and dry slightly. Repeat until you have 6 matching napkin rings. Sand rough edges and then add painted decoration and varnish.

tea time

These fun fridge magnets are a crafty way of jazzing up your fridge door and also make a great housewarming gift.

YOU WILL NEED
~

¼ quantity of dough

Templates

Gouache paint

Brushes

Medium grade sandpaper

Rolling pin

Sharp knife

Small magnets

Epoxy resin glue

Varnish

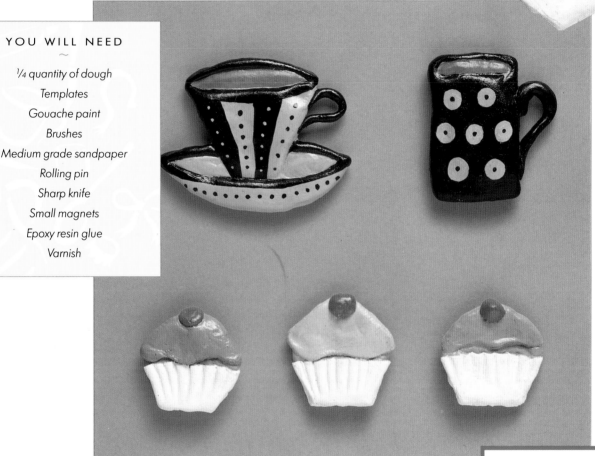

Roll out the dough to 5 mm (¼ in) thickness. Cut out shapes using templates on page 105. To give relief to the shapes add a second layer of dough by cutting the shaded parts of the templates again and laying them over the first piece. Add any relief detail to the shapes before cooking as follows: 5 minutes low; 5 minutes medium low; 1 minute medium; 1 minute medium. Allow resting time out of the microwave between each cooking phase, and check for air bubbles. Sand down any rough edges, then paint and varnish before sticking magnets to the back to finish off.

tip

Make perfect circles by painting the whole shape the colour of the dots then masking with stick-on dots before you paint over with the background colour.

nursery initials

These dough initials have been given an extra touch with the snake-like faces on each one.

YOU WILL NEED

~

Small amount of dough
(depending on number of initials)

Rolling pin

Microwave-safe plate

Cooling tray

Poster paints

Brushes • Varnish

Permanent marker pen

Cocktail stick or similar

Double-sided adhesive pads

Break off a small amount of dough and roll out into a sausage about 1 cm (½ in) diameter. On a microwave-safe plate, bend the sausage into a letter about 9 cm (3½ in) high. Shape one end to a point for the tail and the other to make the mouth of the snake. Make 2 tiny balls of dough and press into the head with the cocktail stick to make the eyes. Cooking 3 letters at a time, cook as follows – 3 to 4 minutes on low, 5 minutes on medium low, 1 minute on medium. Allow the shapes to cool outside the microwave between each phase. Paint each snake a different colour. Use the permanent marker to add zigzags or spots and varnish. Fix to the door or a plaque with the self-adhesive pads.

fruit and flower plaques

These pretty plaques make ideal decorative additions to plain picture frames or mirrors.

Roll out the dough to 5 mm (¼ in) thickness and cut 2 or 3 leaf shapes to form the base of each plaque. Arrange together on a microwave-safe plate. Cut a few ivy leaves and score the veins then lay them on top of your leaf base. Add fruit shapes or flowers to build up a complete plaque – you may need to use a little water as glue. Cook 3 together as follows – 3 minutes medium low, 4 minutes medium high – the cooking time will vary quite widely depending on how much surface detail and thickness you have added to the dough, so watch these carefully and ensure that they are evenly arranged in the oven. Leave to cool between each phase. Add colour and varnish to finish.

MAKING ROSES

Cut out small half-moon or crescent shapes from rolled-out dough. Flatten a crescent in your fingers and roll up to form the centre of the flower or a bud. Add more flattened crescents to build up the flower.

valentine hearts

Make a valentine with a difference for your loved one.

Roll out the dough to 5 mm (¼ in) thickness and use the templates on page 105 to cut out the large and small heart shapes. Transfer to a microwave-safe plate. For the smaller hearts, cut with the canapé cutter; the larger heart features freehand hearts stuck on top to make a relief pattern. Use the bodkin to cut a hole for the ribbon in each shape. Cook as follows: 5 minutes medium low; then 3 minutes medium. Allow to cool between times and flatten out any air bubbles. Paint and varnish, then thread a length of ribbon through the hole in the top of each shape to hang.

YOU WILL NEED

~

¼ quantity of dough

Sharp knife

Rolling pin

Template

Microwave-safe plate

Cooling rack

Bodkin

Small heart-shaped canapé cutters

Gouache paints

Brushes

Satin ribbons

Varnish

ivy leaf dish

This pretty little trinket dish may prove so irresistible that you decide never to give it away!

YOU WILL NEED
~

¼ quantity of dough

Rolling pin

Ivy leaf icing cutter

Sharp knife

Small microwave-safe bowl as mould

Water

Gouache paint

Brushes

Varnish

Roll out the dough to 5 mm (¼ in) thickness and lift over the upturned mould. Smooth the dough down over the sides gently – the advantage of using a clear glass bowl is that you can see any air bubbles trapped underneath. Using the sharp knife and resting your hand on a guide, turn the bowl to trim the dough level. Knock down the cut edge with the blade of the knife to make a smooth finish. Cut leaf shapes and fix to the edge of the bowl so that the leaves overlap slightly – use a little water as glue. Mark the leaves with veins, then cook as follows: 3 minutes medium low repeatedly until completely dry; leave the bowl to rest and cool between phases. Once the dough is dry, knock the bowl gently from the mould and leave the inside to dry fully by giving the bowl a further 3 minutes on medium low and leaving to stand. Paint and varnish to finish.

celestial inspiration

These moon and sun shapes are charming wall plaques and will cost a fraction of the price of their plaster-cast counterparts.

YOU WILL NEED
~

½ quantity of dough

Sharp knife

Rolling pin

Template

Small plate

Cooling rack

Greaseproof paper

Small pear-drop shape canapé cutter

Gold poster paint

Wooden or metal spoon

Varnish

Brushes

Wire

Double-sided adhesive stickers

tip

If you place plaques on greaseproof paper they can be lifted on to a wire rack more easily to dry both back and front in the resting periods.

MOON

Roll out the dough to about 1 cm (½ in) thickness. Use the template on page 105 to make the basic crescent. Use your fingers to smooth off the edges. Add features on top and smooth out joins. Shape the surface of the moon using the back of a wooden or metal spoon. Cook as follows: 5 minutes on medium low; 3 minutes on medium; 1 minute on medium high at intervals until dry. Paint the surface gold then varnish. You can add a small wire loop or use double-sided adhesive stickers to display.

SUN

Roll out the dough to 5 mm (¼ in) thickness and cut out a circle using a small plate as a guide. Cut small peardrop-shaped pieces with the canapé cutter and fix these around the edge of the circle, pinching the ends to make flame effects. Repeat with a second row to fill in the spaces. Cut another circle of dough the same size as the first, and press this on top to hide the joins between the flames and the sun. Mould the features with the remaining dough, building up the eye as shown with a ball of dough and a crescent-shaped piece for the eyelid. Cook as follows: 8 minutes on medium low; 3 minutes on medium; then 1 to 2 minute intervals on medium until dry. Paint, then finish off with several coats of varnish.

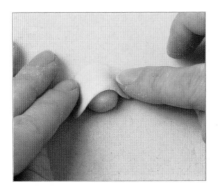

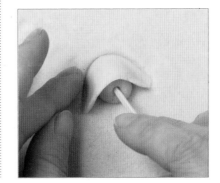

floral frames

A perfect gift for family and friends in which to display a treasured photograph.

YOU WILL NEED

~

½ quantity of dough

Rolling pin

Template

Microwave-safe plate

Water • Cooling rack

Knife • Ivy leaf icing cutter

Stiff card

Clear acetate sheet

Double-sided sticky tape

Gouache paint

Brushes • Varnish

Picture • Cord

ROSES FRAME

Roll out the dough to 5 mm (¼ in) thickness and cut out the frame using the template on page 105. Place on a microwave-safe plate. Cut leaves and press into place, then add thin sausages as stalks. Make roses and rose buds as shown on page 17 and use small amounts of water to glue these in place. Make a bow as for the napkins on page 21 and place this on top to finish. Cook as follows: 5 minutes on medium low followed by 5 minutes on medium. Watch the decoration carefully for scorching and reduce back to medium low if this appears. Paint and varnish the frame. To complete the frame cut a piece of card to make a backing and a slightly smaller sized piece of acetate to make the "glass". Stick double-sided tape around three sides of the card leaving the top open and stick this to the back of the frame. Slot in your picture with the acetate "glass". Make a stand with card or stick a loop of cord to the back to hang the frame up.

ARCHED FRAME

Roll a sausage about 1.5 cm (⅝ in) in diameter and 40 cm (16 in) long. Place on a microwave-safe plate in an arched shape with the base about 12 cm (5 in) wide. Roll out the remaining dough to 5 mm (¼ in) thickness and use to decorate the frame with ivy leaves and flowers. Dry in a similar way to the rose frame. Paint and varnish then add a cardboard back, acetate "glass" and a hanging loop to finish.

a n i m a l   m a g i c

These hard-wearing shapes are excellent nursery toys and make a great start for a Noah's Ark or zoo collection.

tip

You could colour the shapes in groups to make them into a matching and sorting game.

YOU WILL NEED
~

¼ quantity of dough

Rolling pin

Templates

Microwave-safe plate

Sharp knife

Medium grade sandpaper

Gouache

Brushes • Varnish

Thin card

Green sticky-backed plastic

Doubled-sided sticky tape

Roll out the dough to 5 mm (¼ in) thickness. Using the templates on page 106 cut out the animal shapes. Arrange evenly on a microwave-safe plate and cook as follows: 5 minutes low; 5 minutes medium low; 1 minute medium; 1 minute medium – allowing the dough to stand between phases. Once the dough is dry, sand off any rough edges. Paint on the base colour then leave to dry before adding any other markings. Varnish. Make stands by cutting pieces of thin card 5 cm (2 in) square. Fold the squares in half down the middle, then fold edges back up to the centre fold. Join at the centre fold with double-sided tape, then open up the outer folds. Cover with sticky-backed plastic. Fix to the animal shapes with glue or double-sided tape so the animals stand up.

TIE AND DYE

~ 3 ~

*t*he transformation of plain fabrics by masking areas before they come into contact with dyes is an ancient technique, and the tying off of areas is one of the simplest ways to carry it out. Here we use both fabrics and yarns with water-soluble dyes in the microwave to achieve fast results without standing over a boiling pan on the stove. We used Dylon Hand dye – a permanent colour designed for natural fabrics.

FABRIC DYEING

Tie-dyeing a piece of fabric is quite a straightforward process although the final outcome of the dyeing is never totally predictable. This is because you have little control over the areas of fabric which come into contact with the colour. However, through the use of various knots and bindings, you can make an approximation of the final pattern – see the guide on page 31.

The fabric is manipulated, bound or sewn so that during the dyeing process some parts do not come into contact with the colour – this is known as using a resist. It is the combination of the coloured and undyed areas along with the variety in colour penetration due to the binding or knotting which creates the patterns in the dyed fabric. The patterned fabric can then be used to enhance your craft projects using the stripes or spirals to accentuate the shape or design of the item you are making. Many of the projects in this book use just one dye colour although there is no reason why you should not redye the item to create the variety of colour in the cafetière cover on page 39. The overall effect is created by the knotting, the choice of colour or colours and the shape of the final project which the fabric is used for.

There is no reason why you should not dye finished garments in your microwave, but check that there are no metal parts. The silk shirt, child's T-shirt and the long scarf all started as cream or off-white garments.

> ### tip
>
> Fabrics most suitable for dyeing in the microwave: silk, cotton (including calico) and linen. Yarns suitable for dyeing in the microwave: cotton, silk and linen.

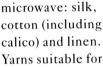

DYEING YARNS

Dyeing an entire hank or part of a hank of yarn in the microwave oven before knitting, weaving or crocheting is a very simple process. Masking of the area of yarn not to be coloured is achieved by simply keeping that part of the hank out of the dye bath or by knotting. By altering the length of the hank, the yarn can be dyed any number of separate colours before being made up into the rainbow effect in the baby items on page 34.

tie-dye fabric

YOU WILL NEED

~

Dye – Dylon Hand which contains Azo Reactive Dyes

Large glass bowl

Water

Washing powder

Plastic bag

Rubber gloves

Yarn or fabric

Scissors

String, cord or strong thread for knots and bindings

Marbles or pieces of cork to tie into fabric

Measuring jug

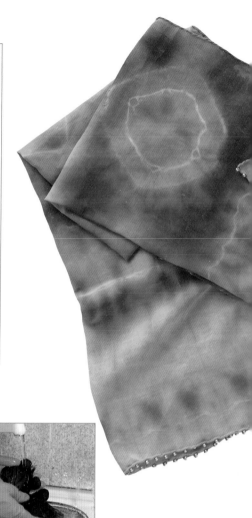

1 MIX THE DYE POWDER WITH 500 ML (1 PT) OF WATER IN THE GLASS BOWL AND SQUEEZE THE SOLUTION THROUGH THE PREPARED FABRIC. THE AMOUNT OF FABRIC YOU CAN DYE AT ONE TIME DEPENDS VERY MUCH ON THE BULK. IT IS OFTEN ADVANTAGEOUS TO CUT THE FABRIC MORE OR LESS TO SIZE BEFORE DYEING SO THAT THE PATTERN SUITS THE SIZE OF THE FINISHED ARTICLE.

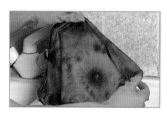

2 COVER THE BOWL OR PLACE IN A PLASTIC BAG AND COOK ON HIGH FOR 4 MINUTES. REMOVE AND RINSE IN COLD WATER.

3 ONCE THE WATER RUNS CLEAR, REMOVE ALL KNOTS AND TIES AND WASH THOROUGHLY USING HOT WATER AND WASHING POWDER. RINSE AND DRY.

knotting guide

Picking up the fabric from the centre and tying at regular intervals gives you a spider's web effect.

Randomly knotting in pieces of cork or marbles at the centre then gathering up the corners gives this effect.

Scrunching up the fabric tightly in a random ball gives an all-over pattern.

Pleating the fabric across its width then knotting at regular intervals gives a regular pattern like this.

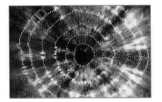

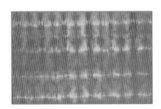

DYEING YARN

1 MIX THE DYE POWDER WITH 500 ML (1 PT) OF WATER IN THE GLASS BOWL AND SQUEEZE THE SOLUTION THROUGH THE PREPARED YARN. TYING THE YARN IN HANKS OF ABOUT 25 G (1 OZ) ENSURES THAT THE DYE IS THOROUGHLY ABSORBED ALL THE WAY THROUGH THE HANK.

2 COVER THE BOWL OR PLACE IN A PLASTIC BAG AND COOK ON HIGH FOR 4 MINUTES.

3 RINSE THE YARN IN COLD WATER, REMOVING ALL KNOTS AND TIES ONCE THE WATER RUNS CLEAR, AND WASH THROUGH USING WASHING POWDER AND HOT WATER. RINSE AND DRY.

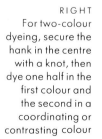

LEFT
For a shaded one-colour dye, simply knot the hank of yarn in the centre.

RIGHT
For two-colour dyeing, secure the hank in the centre with a knot, then dye one half in the first colour and the second in a coordinating or contrasting colour

pretty pouches

Made from small pieces of white silk, these colourful pouches are ideal for carrying make-up or cotton wool.

YOU WILL NEED
~

30 cm (12 in) of 90 cm (36 in) wide fine silk makes 2 pouches

1 m (39 in) fine coloured ribbon for each pouch

Dye

Knotting thread

Needle and thread

Fabric glue

tip

Use fabric glue instead of sewing the pouches if your needle skills are a bit rusty.

Cut the width of fabric in half to make 2 rectangles. Pleat each from the selvedge in 2 cm (¾ in) wide pleats, then tie tightly in bands at 3 cm (1¼ in) intervals halfway down the length. Tie the bottom half in a random ball. Dye and treat the prepared fabric as shown and described in the step-by-step instructions on page 30.

Cut out a pattern piece using the template on page 106. Cut this on a straight fold with the stripes in the dyed fabric to the top. Stitch the straight seam together and extend the seam down to the first point. Then stitch from the base of the folded edge to the point. Open up and refold the bag to match the remaining raw edges at the bottom and then stitch across. Fold over the top along the fold line to the inside and stitch a casing. Thread ribbon through the casing and draw up by making a small opening in the seam on the right side of the pouch.

~ P R O J E C T ~

basket bonus

Little wicker baskets are made extra special with these padded tie-dyed liners and are ideal for keeping bread warm on the table.

YOU WILL NEED
~

Small baskets

Cotton fabric – calculated as below

Wadding – calculated as below

Paper to make patterns

Dye

Knotting thread

Sewing equipment

Make pattern pieces for your basket by measuring around the top of the basket and the depth to calculate a size for the side panel and drawing around the base of the basket for the bottom piece. If you want to make a lid, draw around the top of the basket too. Add 1.5 cm (⅝ in) for a seam allowance and cut out the paper pieces. To calculate the amount of fabric to dye you will need 2 side panels, 2 base panels and 2 lid panels. You will also need light-weight wadding for the base, sides and lid. Before dyeing, knot marbles, pebbles or corks randomly into the fabric pieces then treat as described in the step-by-step instructions on page 30.

Cut out all the pieces you need. Place the base wadding between the base pieces to make a sandwich and tack them together. Match the side-panel pieces with the wadding in the same way then stitch the short seam to make a complete circle. Trim down the wadding in the seam turnings and fold the raw edges of seam allowances over to make a neat edge and stitch again. Match one of the long sides of the side panel to the base, easing the excess fabric evenly all round. Tack and machine. Neaten in a similar way to the side seam. Cut a bias binding in left-over fabric and bind the top edge of the basket liner.

Make the lid by making a sandwich of the dyed fabric panels and wadding as for the base and sides and finish off the edges with bias binding.

tip

Use ready-made bias binding in a contrasting colour for speed.

~ P R O J E C T ~

boxing clever

These fabric boxes fold flat in a drawer when not in use. Owing to the extra stiff interfacing used, they are fully washable.

YOU WILL NEED

~

*Two squares of fabric 25 cm
(10 in) by 25 cm (10 in) for
each box*

Stiff interfacing

Contrast bias binding

Dye

Knotting thread

Sewing equipment

Pleat the fabric panels tightly then tie at 2 cm (¾ in) intervals. Dye and treat as described in the step-by-step instructions on page 30. Lay 2 fabric panels wrong sides together and tack to hold them straight. Machine a line of stitches 5 cm (2 in) in from one of the straight edges. Repeat on the opposite edge. Turn the fabric square 45 degrees and machine another line of stitches 5 cm (2 in) in from a raw edge.

Cut panels of interfacing to fit the rectangular side pocket you have created – you will need altogether 4 rectangles for the 4 sides and you will also need a central 15 cm (6 in) square panel to fit into the centre section of the box. Slot all the pieces of interfacing into position and machine the final straight seam 5 cm (2 in) in from the last edge to complete the square. Trim the corners on the diagonal then finish off the raw edges with bias binding all round. Fix ribbon ties to the 8 seam ends and then tie them to make the box.

baby bliss

The random effect of dyed cotton yarn when knitted up adds to the charm of these simple baby knits. The method for dyeing the cotton yarn for this project is shown and explained on page 31.

YOU WILL NEED
~

100 g (4 oz) of cotton yarn
Two colours of dye
Pair 4 mm (No. 8) knitting needles
Coordinating satin ribbons
Scissors
Bodkin
Dyed yarn in two colours

TO KNIT UP

Check tension – 18 stitches and 27 rows on 4 mm (No. 8) needles = 10 cm (4 in) square.

Waistcoat Back

Cast on 38 stitches then work in garter stitch for 8 rows. Switch to stocking stitch for 12 cm (5 in), then work the first and last 10 stitches of each row in garter stitch for the next 5 rows. Cast off 7 stitches at the beginning of the next 2 rows. Continue to work straight, working the first and last 3 stitches of each row in garter stitch until the work measures 22 cm (8¾ in) from the cast-on edge. Cast off 6 stitches at the beginning of the next 2 rows then work 3 rows of garter stitch with the remaining stitches before casting off.

tip

By dyeing with pink and blue you can hedge your bets and be ready in advance with a gift for a newborn baby.

Waistcoat Front

Cast on 19 stitches and work in garter stitch for the next 8 rows. Work the first 3 stitches of the next row in garter stitch then continue in stocking stitch. Continue working these 3 stitches in garter stitch until the work measures 12 cm (5 in) from the cast-on edge. With the wrong side facing, work garter stitch for the first 10 stitches of the next 5 rows. Cast off 7 stitches at the beginning of the next row then continue working straight with the 3 stitches in garter stitch for 4 rows. With the right side facing, work garter stitch for 3 stitches then decrease one stitch, continue to the end. Work 3 rows. Decrease this way twice more until you have 9 stitches. Work until the front matches the back length, then cast off. Work a reverse version for the other side. Press the pieces. Stitch the fronts and back together at shoulders and side seams then add ribbon ties.

BOOTEES

Using 4 mm (No. 8) needles cast on 4 stitches. First row – knit. Second row – purl. Third row – knit 1, pick up loop to make 1 and knit, knit 2, pick up loop to make 1 and knit, knit 1 – total 6 stitches. Fourth row – purl. Fifth row – knit 2 pick up loop and knit to make 1, knit 2, pick up loop and knit to make 1, knit to end. Sixth row – knit 3 stitches, pick up and knit loop to make 1 and knit, knit 2, pick up loop to make 1 and knit, work to end. Seventh row – purl. Continue increasing and pattern until there are 28 stitches on the needle. Next row – purl to the centre of work then turn and knit. Work these 14 stitches for 11 rows. Cast off the first 4 stitches at the beginning of the next row then continue straight for 4 rows. Cast off. Return to the remaining stitches and rejoin yarn. Work the other side of the bootee as a mirror image of the first. Cast off. With the right side facing, pick up and knit 32 stitches around the ankle edge (the "seam" where your increased stitches will fall in the centre of this edge). Work in garter stitch for 9 rows. Cast off. Work the second bootee in the same way.

Stitch the sole and heel seam then match to make the base of the heel. Thread ribbon through the ankle and tie.

covered in style

This simple cot blanket shows how effective the use of one-colour yarn dyeing can be.

> ## YOU WILL NEED
> ~
> *300 g (12 oz) of knitting yarn*
> *4 mm (No. 8) needles*
> *Dye*
> *Coordinating 2.5 cm (1 in) satin ribbons*

TO KNIT UP

Dye the yarn by knotting in the centre (see page 31).

Cast on 70 stitches. Work in garter stitch for 6 rows. Next row, work the first 5 stitches in garter, then 10 in stocking, then 10 in garter, repeat 10 stocking, 10 garter to the last 5, work these in garter. Repeat for 16 rows to make alternate garter and stocking-stitch panels with garter edging, then reverse the blocks to make a chequerboard effect. Work for 10 blocks then work the last 6 rows across in garter stitch and cast off. Press flat. Make two-tone bows by joining 2 10 cm (4 in) lengths of ribbon in the centre and attaching to the corners of the blanket before tying in bows.

pride of place

Making an individual place mat and napkin is a great first project for a youngster.

PREPARATION AND DYEING

To get the same effect as this, pleat fabric into 6 cm (2½ in) wide pleats across its width then tack the layers together in a wide zigzag line using large stitches and strong thread. Pull up the thread tightly and tie the bunches with string. Dye the fabric following the step-by-step instructions on page 30.

TO MAKE UP

Cut the dyed fabric into 2 panels, one measuring 28 cm (11 in) by 40 cm (16 in) (front), one 35 cm (14 in) by 47 cm (18½ in) (back) and 2 strips 5 cm (2 in) by 20 cm (8 in) for napkin ties. Lay the front with the right side up on top of the interfacing panel then place both in the centre of the back piece. Fold a 1.5 cm (⅝ in) hem around the 3.5 cm (1½ in) back border and fold over on to the front to hide the raw edges. Mitre the corners then machine down all round. Make ties and machine to the left of the mat. Cut a square from the remaining fabric to make a napkin and finish off the raw edges before rolling and tying to the mat.

YOU WILL NEED
~

50 cm (20 in) of 90 cm (36 in) wide cream cotton sateen

40 cm (16 in) by 28 cm (11 in) thick interfacing

Dye

Knotting thread

Sewing equipment

coffee cover-up

Keep your fresh coffee warm in style with this bold quilted cover-up made with two-tone dyed fabric.

YOU WILL NEED
~

Around 30 cm (12 in) of 90 cm (36 in) wide cotton sateen fabric

Around 20 cm (8 in) thin polyester wadding

Contrast satin binding

Sewing equipment

Dye

Knotting thread

Paper

PREPARATION AND DYEING

Make a paper template for your cafetière so that the pieces meet at the back and there is a slight dip to allow for the pouring lip at the centre front. Check this against the fabric to be sure you have enough. Tie the fabric in a random ball, and dye (see page 30). We used coloured sateen to get the two-coloured effect, but you could double dye in two different colours and reknot each time.

TO MAKE UP

Cut 2 fabric panels, 1 in wadding and 4 strips of fabric 20 cm (8 in) by 8 cm (3 in) to make the ties (you could use ribbon).

Sandwich the wadding between the dyed fabric with the right sides outside and tack together across the centre and around the edge. Machine straight lines around 2 cm (¾ in) apart starting in the centre and working your way out to quilt the panel. Make ties and position 2 on each side on the right side of the cover at the centre back. Bind raw edges all round with bias binding, machining in ties at the same time.

tip

If you are good at machining, use contrasting thread for the quilting to add to the effect.

crafty comfort

These cushions are simple to make and the
glass-bead edging adds to their ethnic style.

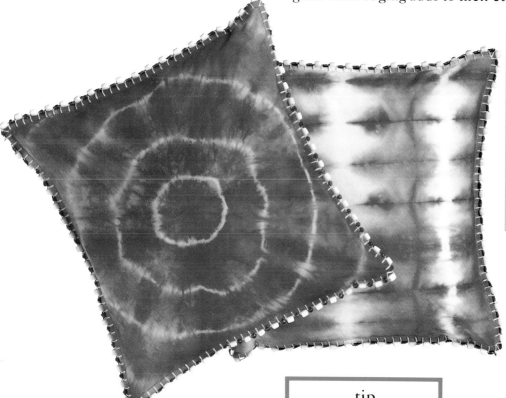

YOU WILL NEED
~
40 cm (16 in) of 90 cm (36 in) wide white fabric
30 cm (12 in) cushion pad
Sewing equipment
Dye
Knotting thread
White embroidery thread
Beads

tip

You could easily dye
ready-made covers
and add your own
beaded decoration.

Tie the fabric in pleats at 2 cm (¾ in) intervals (blue version) or in a pleated
spiral from the centre point then tied at regular intervals (red version). Dye
and treat as shown in the step-by-step instructions on page 30. Cut out 1
front panel 33 cm (13¼ in) square and 2 back pieces 33 cm (13¼ in) by 27
cm (10¾ in). Make up the cover by turning over a hem on one edge of each
of the back pieces then overlapping these on the right side of the front piece
and stitching all round. Turn the cover through the envelope opening you
have made and press. Trim edges with blanket stitch and beads.

personal touch

Make a guest feel extra special by adding a band of coordinating
tie-dyed fabric to a towel and face cloth. The pleated knotting
used here is ideal for the band effect.

YOU WILL NEED

~

Small hand towel and face cloth

*20 cm (8 in) wide strips of white
cotton to match width of towel
plus a seam allowance*

Dye

Knotting thread

Sewing equipment

To get the same effect as this,
pleat the fabric strips in 6 cm
(2½ in) pleats along their length
then again down the length of the
pleated fabric to form a bulky
parcel and bind this very tightly.
Dye, rinse and wash as shown in
the step-by-step instructions on
page 30.

Turn the raw edges of one of the
strips over to make a band and
slip-stitch this in place over the
plain band on the towel. Make a
bow by sewing the long edges
of another strip together and
turning the fabric through
to make a band and
tying into a bow. Use
to trim the towel. With
the remaining fabric, tie the
face cloth with a band and finish
with a bow.

teddy extra

A great way of using up little off-cuts from your projects; this plain teddy has been given an extra touch with fabric pads and a bow tie, making a more personal gift.

tip

Trimming or shaving the fur pile from the pads where you position the fabric will help it to lie flat.

YOU WILL NEED

~

Teddy

Tie-dye remnants

Sewing equipment

Cut 2 triangles, one to cover each ear; 2 rectangles, one for each foot; and 2 squares, one for each paw. Pin each piece roughly in position then slip-stitch in place turning the raw edges in as you go. Make a coordinating bow tie from the remaining fabric and fix it around the neck.

~PROJECT~

silk sensation

Take a plain silk shirt and make it your own with a combination of colour and knotting.

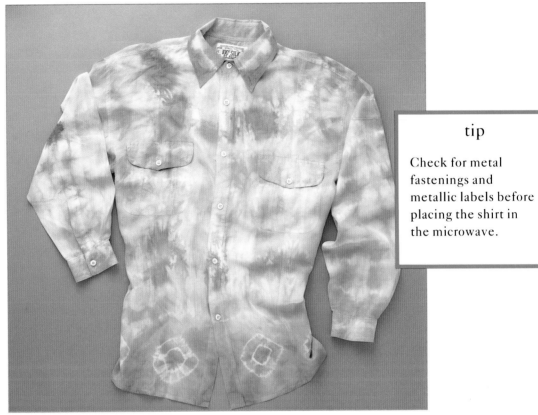

tip

Check for metal fastenings and metallic labels before placing the shirt in the microwave.

YOU WILL NEED
~

Silk shirt

Dye

Knotting thread

For a similar pattern to the one shown, pleat the sleeves lengthways, then knot at regular intervals. Tie a row of pebbles or corks along the hemline of the shirt, spacing them evenly, and tie the front and back of the shirt into a random ball. Dye and treat, as shown in the step-by-step instructions on page 30, then iron well.

retouched t-shirt

This child's T-shirt has been given a new lease of life with a quick treatment in the microwave oven. Ideal for letting those greying whites see another day.

YOU WILL NEED
~
T-shirt
Dye
Knotting thread

For a similar effect to the one shown, pleat and knot the sleeves then pick up the front from the centre and knot in pleats. Repeat for the back. Dye and treat as shown on page 30.

dramatic voile

This ready-finished plain voile scarf has been given the microwave tie-dye treatment to transform it into a stylish accessory.

YOU WILL NEED
~

Cotton voile scarf
Dye
Knotting thread

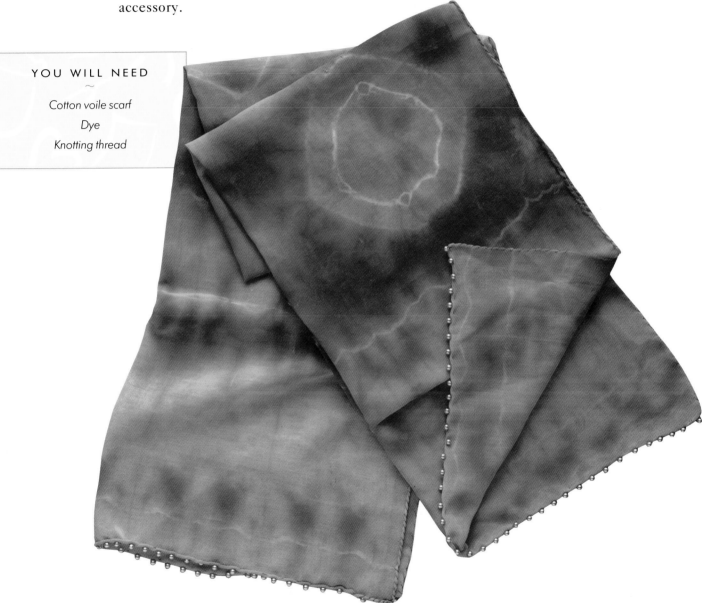

Tie the scarf in pleats along its length leaving a small section at each end to knot into small circles. Dye and treat as shown on page 30. Remember to check that any trimming is non-metallic before dyeing.

ntil recent years papier mâché was thought by many to belong in the classroom, with sticky balloons and greased china saucers acting as moulds for childrens' first creative steps with paper and paste. However, it is an ancient craft based on layers of pasted paper or paper pulp that were used back in the earliest of paper-making cultures in China in AD2.

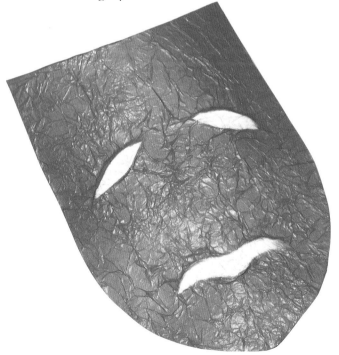

The versatility of papier mâché can be seen in the projects developed here for you to copy. Inexpensive to create, light in weight and easy to handle, once dried papier mâché is a hard, resilient material. It was even used for furniture in Europe and America in the 19th century. Whether you are working in paper pulp or strips, the shaping and moulding process gradually builds up the shape you want; and after drying a coat of white gesso and colourful decoration soon disguises the humble beginnings of your craft work.

As with the other crafts in this book, the microwave oven may at one time limit your creativity owing to its size while at another it may make your experiments all the more diverse because of the speed with which you can get your results.

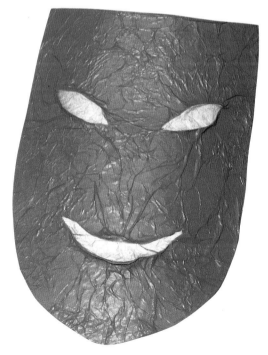

making papier mâché

STRIP METHOD

1 TEAR THE NEWSPAPER INTO STRIPS ABOUT 5 CM (2 IN) WIDE AND 15 CM (6 IN) LONG.

4 REMOVE FROM THE MOULD WHEN COOL AND TRIM THE EDGE.

2 PASTE BOTH SIDES OF THE STRIPS WITH WALLPAPER PASTE AND START TO BUILD UP THE SHAPE. USE A MICROWAVE-SAFE MOULD COVERED WITH CLEAR FOOD WRAP TO EASE REMOVAL.

5 PASTE SMALL STRIPS OVER THE CUT EDGE AND DRY ON HIGH FOR 1 MINUTE. LEAVE UNTIL HARD. COAT THE FINISHED SHAPE WITH GESSO TO SEAL BEFORE DECORATING.

3 WHEN YOU HAVE BUILT UP 6 TO 8 LAYERS OF PASTED PAPER, COOK THE PAPIER MÂCHÉ ON MEDIUM HIGH FOR 1 TO 2 MINUTES, TAKE OUT AND STAND UNTIL IT STOPS STEAMING AND REPEAT UNTIL DRY.
USE THE STANDING TIME TO PRESS OUT ANY AIR BUBBLES.

PULP METHOD

1 TEAR THE NEWSPAPER INTO PIECES ABOUT 2 CM (¾ IN) SQUARE AND PLACE IN A MICROWAVE-SAFE BOWL.

2 FILL THE BOWL WITH BOILING WATER.

3 MICROWAVE ON HIGH FOR 10 MINUTES THEN STIR AND LEAVE TO STAND FOR 30 MINUTES. REPEAT 5 TO 6 TIMES UNTIL THE PAPER DISINTEGRATES.

4 SQUEEZE OUT ALL EXCESS WATER THROUGH A COLANDER OR SIEVE.

5 MIX THE PAPER PULP WITH WALLPAPER PASTE UNTIL IT FORMS A MASHED-POTATO-LIKE CONSISTENCY.

6 PREPARE A MOULD BY COVERING IT IN CLEAR FOOD WRAP THEN SPREAD THE PULP EVENLY OVER THE MOULD.

7 COOK ON MEDIUM LOW FOR 5 MINUTE INTERVALS WITH 5 MINUTES STANDING TIME BETWEEN. GRADUALLY INCREASE THE COOKING POWER TO MEDIUM HIGH UNTIL THE PULP IS TOTALLY DRY. COAT THE FINISHED SHAPE WITH GESSO AS FOR THE STRIP METHOD BEFORE DECORATING.

safety

The paper can scorch if over-cooked so keep an eye on the drying process at all times. It is important that you remove the papier mâché from the oven in between the periods of cooking to allow the steam to disperse. You may find that the inside of the oven benefits from wiping out too.

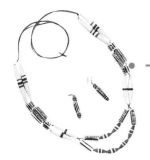

ethnic beads

These beads and matching earrings are made by simply rolling tapering lengths of pasted paper around wooden skewers into bead shapes.

YOU WILL NEED

~

Cartridge paper

Scissors

Wallpaper paste

Wooden skewers or cocktail sticks

Microwave-safe plate

Gesso

Coloured paint

Paint brushes

Varnish

Fine cord

Wire earring hooks

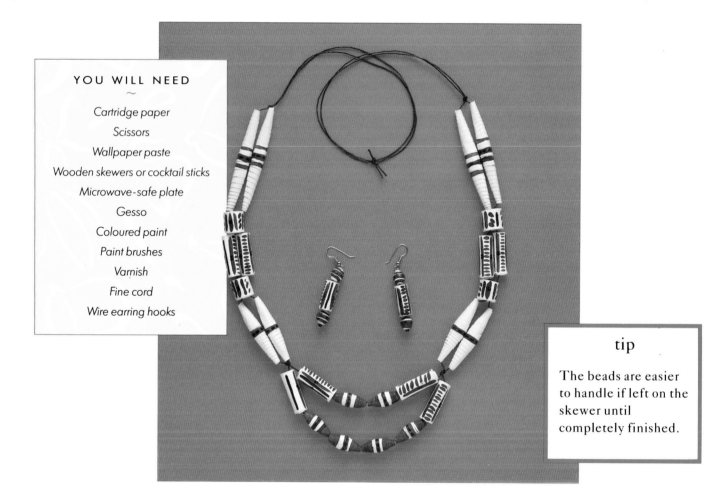

tip

The beads are easier to handle if left on the skewer until completely finished.

Cut the cartridge paper into triangles approximately 30 cm (12 in) long and varying from 2 to 7 cm (¾ to 2¾ in) wide at the base to make different sized beads. Paste all but the first 2 cm (¾ in) of the triangle at the wide end then roll over the skewer. Remove and place on a microwave-safe plate, then repeat to make the number of beads you want. Cook for 30-second bursts on medium high, and stand until the beads are dry. Decorate and varnish. String on to fine cord to make the necklace or use wire earring hooks to make the matching earrings.

bracelet and brooches

This eye-catching bracelet with matching brooches is bound to make you the envy of your friends.

YOU WILL NEED
~

Newspaper

Wallpaper paste

Steel rule

Clear food wrap

Round mould – a milk bottle or something similar is good

Scissors

Gesso

Paint brushes

Paint and varnish to decorate

Steel pins

BRACELET

Cover the mould with clear food wrap, then paste and stick long strips of paper in a spiral around the mould. Cook on medium high and stand until the collar of the papier mâché is dry, then slide off. Seal the cut edges with short paper strips. Dry before sealing with gesso and decorating.

BROOCHES

Stick together six circles of pasted paper. Fold into shape before drying, sealing and decorating. Add the steel pins last.

hat pins

These colourful pins will make a stylish addition to a plain hat.

YOU WILL NEED

~

Thin card

Templates

Masking tape

Newspaper

Wallpaper paste

Steel rule

Gesso

Paint brushes

Paint and varnish to decorate

Hat pins

Make a card mould of the basic half-hat shape using the templates on page 109, and stick together with small pieces of masking tape. Cover in strips of pasted paper leaving the back open so that you can slot in the hat pin, cook on medium high, and dry gently.

Make the bow using cut strips of paper, 2 short lengths to make the ribbon ends and a long length looped and pinched together to make the bow part. Cook on medium high, and dry. Stick the bow to the finished hat before sealing with gesso and decorating. Add the hat pin.

shaker-style boxes

These classic boxes can be reproduced both cheaply and quickly from moulds made from thin card.

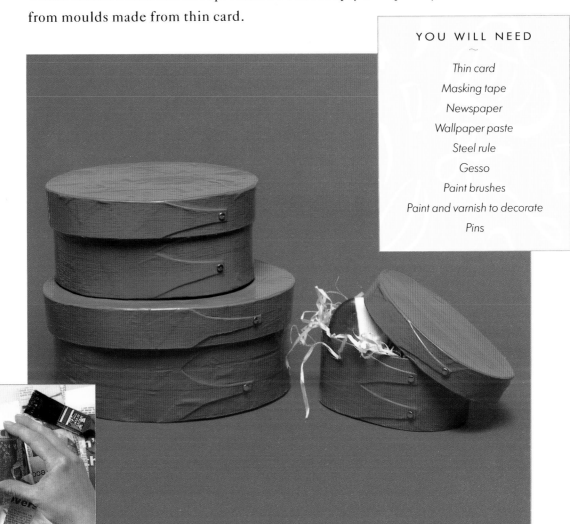

Make a copy of a Shaker box and lid using the fine card and masking tape, and the templates on page 107 as a guide. Using strips of pasted paper, build up the surface until there are 6 to 8 layers to give the box strength. Cook on medium high, and dry. Seal with gesso, and paint in Shaker-style colours. Add small dots of colour to resemble the tacks, or use real pins. Varnish.

layered bowls

Use either the inside or outside surface of the bowl for the mould and add decoration to suit.

YOU WILL NEED
~

Microwave-safe bowls to use as moulds

Clear food wrap

Newspaper

Wallpaper paste

Scissors

Masking tape

Steel rule

Gesso

Paint brushes

Paint and varnish to decorate

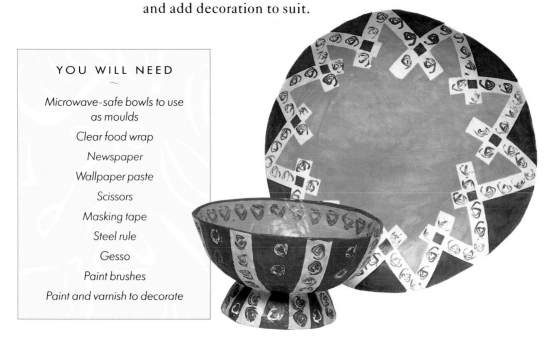

masking and paper stamp pattern

Cover the inside surface of the bowls with clear food wrap, then layers of pasted strips of newspaper extending up over the side. Cook on medium high, and dry. Remove the paper bowl from the mould and cut the edge level with scissors.

To make a stand make a second paper bowl and cut it down further. Then turn it upside down and tape the two together. Add layers of pasted newspaper to strengthen the join. Dry in the usual way, watching out for scorching. Seal with gesso and decorate.

p u l p   b o w l

This bowl uses the pulp method to give an uneven surface to the
finished bowl, enhanced by the painted finish.

YOU WILL NEED
~

Newspaper

Microwave-safe bowl

Colander or sieve

Clear food wrap

Wallpaper paste

Scissors

Gesso

Brush

Paint and varnish

Sponge

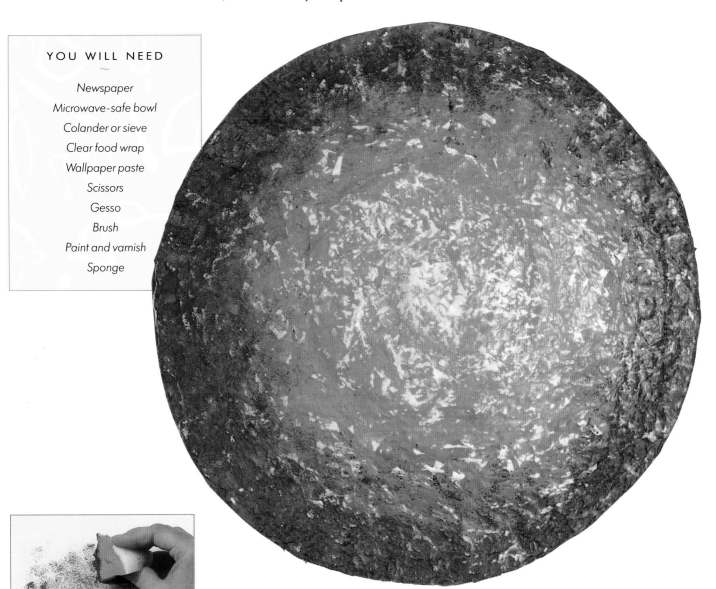

Make a quantity of pulp papier mâché, then spread it evenly
over the surface of the prepared bowl mould. Cook slowly on
medium low, and dry out. Remove the dry bowl from the
mould, and trim the edge even. Seal with gesso all over, then sponge paint
colour on as shown, to get the mottled effect. Finish with varnish.

jugs

These colourful jugs are made by using a thin card mould and strips of newspaper to reinforce the finished container.

YOU WILL NEED

~

Thin card

Masking tape

Newspaper

Wallpaper paste

Steel rule

Gesso

Paint brushes

Paint and varnish to decorate

Make a card mould of a jug, including a rough handle and lip, using the templates on page 109. Paste strips of newspaper all over the moulds until they are 6 to 8 layers thick, then cook on medium high, and dry out. Seal the finished jugs with gesso before decorating and varnishing.

tick-tock clock

This clock is based on a platter of pulp-method papier mâché. A simple bought clock mechanism is added to make a stylish timepiece.

YOU WILL NEED
~

Pulp papier mâché
Card
Cooling rack
Gesso
Poster paints
Battery clock mechanism
Flat microwave-safe platter
Clear food wrap

Prepare the pulp, then cover the platter with a layer of clear food wrap. Spread the pulp evenly over the platter in the shape of the clock face. Build up a foot at one end for the clock to stand on (or add a card stand afterwards). Cook on medium low for 10 minutes, bring out, and cool. Continue for 10 minutes on medium. Continue on medium with cooling periods until dry. Remove the clock face from the platter and cool it on a wire cooling rack. Seal it with gesso, then paint the face using the masking method. Pierce a hole through the centre and position the clock parts.

l a m p s h a d e

A delicate punched edging and bow details make a pretty
lampshade for the home.

YOU WILL NEED
~

*Two large sheets of fine textured
wrapping paper*

Assorted coordinating fine ribbon

Wallpaper paste

Pasting brush

Large bowl for mould

Scissors

Hole punch

Clear food wrap

Cover the inside of the bowl with clear food wrap. Tear
the wrapping paper as you would for strip method papier
mâché, paste and layer on to the inside of the bowl
until it is completely and evenly covered. Cook on
medium high for short bursts until dry, then leave
to cool. Pierce a hole through the centre for the
flex, then trim the edge into shallow scallops.
Using the hole punch, add the detail around the
edge. Stick on small ribbon bows all round.

safety

Do not use a light
bulb in excess of 60
watt with this shade.

basket with bows

You'll never be stuck for a container for a gift with this clever papier mâché basket based on the strip method.

YOU WILL NEED
~

Newspaper

Wallpaper paste

Ruler

Brushes

Gesso

Coloured paints

Varnish

Oval casserole as mould

Thin card

Double-sided tape

Clear food wrap

Scissors.

Cover the inside of the oval dish with clear food wrap then build up 6 to 8 layers of pasted strips of newspaper extending over the top of the dish. Cook on medium high in 30 second bursts, allowing the steam to dry off, until the papier mâché is dry. Remove from the dish and trim the edge level all round. Cut a 2 cm (¾ in) wide strip of card to make the handle and tape in place, then cover the cut edge of the dish and handle with small strips of newspaper. Make a paper bow in the same way as shown for the hat pin on page 52 and stick it into position before drying again. Seal with gesso, then paint and varnish.

happy and sad masks

If you use thin card as a base,
these masks will be tough
enough to wear or hang.

YOU WILL NEED
~

Fine card

Newspaper

Wallpaper paste

Scissors

Pencil

Blue tissue paper

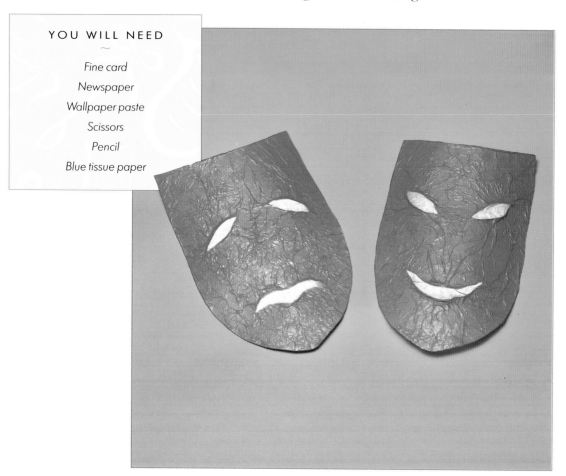

Cut out the mask shapes in the thin card using the template on page 110.
Cover with two to three layers of newspaper strips; you can add to the relief
by adding extra around the eyes and mouth at this stage if you wish. Cook
on medium high for bursts of 30 seconds, allowing to steam, and continue
till dry. Cover the front of the mask with an even layer of wallpaper paste,
then lay a crumpled sheet of coloured tissue paper on top. Fold the tissue
round to the back of the mask and stick it in place.

~ P R O J E C T ~

t a l l   p o t

You can make this large container using a microwave-safe vase as
a mould.

YOU WILL NEED
~

Newspaper

Wallpaper paste

Microwave-safe mould (vase)

Clear food wrap

Craft knife

Thin card

Masking tape

Gesso

Coloured paints

Paint brushes

Varnish

Cover the vase in clear food wrap
then paste 6 to 8 layers of strips of
newspaper evenly all over the
vase, covering the base and sides
completely. Dry off in the
microwave as usual.

With the craft knife, cut down the side of the vase until the shape narrows again, around above the base and then up to the neck again.

Carefully separate the cut panel from the mould and lift away the other section.

Put the two parts of the papier mâché vase together again with masking tape and add a collar made from thin card.

Paste strips of paper over the join and the collar to strengthen them. Dry out in the microwave for short bursts of 30 seconds on medium high with standing time of 1 minute, watching for scorching all the time. Coat the finished shape with gesso.

The surface effect was created with a pad of scrunched newspaper dipped in paint to create a random paint application, and repeated in several colours before sealing with varnish. **This vase is not waterproof.**

fluted dish I

Creating a sophisticated shape like this handkerchief-edged dish is simpler than you may think.

YOU WILL NEED
~

Tall glass or jar

Scissors

Newspaper

Wallpaper paste

Clear food wrap

Brushes

Gesso

Paint

Varnish

tip

To mould the bowl, place the centre of the pasted triangles in the centre of an upturned glass and fold down over the sides.

Cover the bottom of the glass or jar with clear food wrap to make the mould. Cut six to eight large equilateral triangles in newspaper and paste them together with wallpaper paste. Mould the shape (see box). Cook to dry in short 30-second bursts on high, allowing it to steam in between. Remove the bowl from mould and finish off the edge with short strips of pasted paper. Seal with gesso, paint and varnish.

fluted dish II

Moulding and shaping layers of pasted paper before drying gives this shallow dish a more interesting shape. It has an added relief pattern made with string.

YOU WILL NEED
~

Microwave-safe pudding basin
Newspaper
Wallpaper paste
Clear food wrap
Corks
Scissors
Brushes
Gesso
Paint
Varnish
String
Sponge

tip

Fluting is achieved by carefully pulling away the newspaper from the sides of the bowl.

Line the inside of the pudding basin with clear food wrap. Paste on 6 to 8 layers of newspaper strips as you would for a standard strip papier mâché bowl. Pull the paper layers away from the sides of the basin to make four pockets; you can use corks to hold them away if you like. Dry carefully but quickly on medium high, reshaping if needed as the bowl dries out. Remove the bowl from the mould and trim the edge level, then finish with pasted strips as before. Dry and coat with gesso. Glue on rolls and coils of string before coating with the base colour, then sponge with silver and varnish.

cut-edge platter

The treatment of the edge and a painted pattern make what
would otherwise be a very plain plate much more attractive.

Cover the inside surface of the dish with clear food wrap, then paste on 6 to
8 layers of newspaper strips, continuing over the lip to make an extended
rim. Dry in 30-second bursts on medium high, and allow to steam between.
Remove the platter from the mould once dry and trim the edge to the points
effect of the finished platter. Finish off these cut edges with strips, watch
for them curling slightly with the damp paste. Once dry, coat with gesso
then all over in one colour – navy, for example. Use stick-on stars as masks
before spraying all over in silver paint. Remove the stars to get navy stars on
a silver ground. Add motifs with a silver pen before sealing with varnish.

mobile

By simply repeating the same method to make a number of
shapes you can create your own monochromatic mobile to
fascinate the eye.

YOU WILL NEED
~

Newspaper

Wallpaper paste

Microwave-safe plate

Sewing thread

Fine wire

Brushes

Black-and-white striped wrapping
paper

Gesso

Scissors

Paste together 6 to 8 sheets of newspaper and cut into triangles. Curl each
gummed triangle into a spiral, in a similar way to making the brooches on
page 51. Place on a microwave-safe plate and cook on high in 30-second
bursts. Coat the dried curls with gesso. Cut triangles of striped wrapping
paper the same size as the original newspaper ones and stick these to the
outside edge of the curls. Pierce a small hole in the top of each curl and
suspend with cotton from mobile wires. Hang the mobile in a warm air
stream to let the spirals spin.

DRIED
FLOWERS
~ 5 ~

*d*rying flowers and herbs gives you the colour of fresh blooms throughout the year and allows you to combine flowers from different seasons together in one arrangement. Speeding up the drying process by using the microwave oven is a delicate process and can be carried out either by the open method on a bed of absorbent paper or with the aid of a dessicant which draws the moisture away from the flower or plant. The heat must be very gentle or steam will build up in the plant cells and rupture them. In a very "wet" plant this can have a similar effect to placing a cucumber in the freezer, but all plants will be prone to damage of differing degrees if the heat is too intense. Berried foliage and fleshy flowers such as magnolias are not suitable.

The size of the microwave may limit the length of stem you can dry in one piece although length can be added with wire and tape or dried grass to extend the range of the arrangements you can make. It is also worth hang-drying lengths of grass stem for use with any dried material. Microwave drying may help preserve the colours of some flowers and grasses.

Once dried, the flowers and foliage become a creative tool for you to use in a host of ways with the aid of florists' wires, glue (a glue gun is most useful), floral foam for dried flowers and other discreet additions. The containers and trimmings you choose finish your arrangements.

COLOURS

With a little experimentation you will find that some flowers hold their colour better than others – though, of course, conventionally dried stems are prone to fading and change. Try to use any change in colour to your advantage when creating the arrangement as this is a natural effect and can be used to enhance the overall balance. Some stems such as gypsophila, hydrangeas and some grasses can be coloured using fabric dye in solution to add to the drama of the arrangements while others like eucalyptus and pine cones are particularly suited to colouring with spray paint.

DRYING FLOWERS

Like any new skill, microwave drying of flowers and foliage needs to be careful and controlled. You will need to spend some time experimenting with different techniques and microwave settings until you get to know how your oven copes with the materials involved.

Choosing Flowers and Foliage

Pick flowers just before their peak. Always use dry blooms or stems – not dewy or wet from rain – leave these to dry out in the house before microwaving. Full-blown flowers will often lose their petals after drying. Extra foliage can be added to stems after drying so choose the best heads and pick additional foliage.

DRYING METHODS

There are two main methods of drying plant material in the microwave: open drying; and assisted drying using a hydroscopic (water attracting) agent or desiccant, such as silica gel.

Open Drying

This method can be suitable for herbs, leaves and flowers, although its employment may depend on the use you plan for the materials. It is particularly suited for petals to be used in pot-pourri, or herbs for wreaths, or even for preserving herbs for cooking later in the year. You will also find this an effective way of drying rose buds, as the close nature of the tight bud makes drying with a desiccant more difficult.

Cooking times will vary with the density and quantity of the stems involved. Use a medium to low setting (around 250 watts) and place the plant material on a couple of sheets of absorbent kitchen paper on a microwave-proof plate. The paper will take the moisture from the atmosphere. You may need to change the paper before the stems are dry, and you need to allow resting time for the stems to cool and the water vapour to finish evaporating.

Drying with a Desiccant

This is generally faster and suited to a wider range of plants than open drying. The best desiccant is silica gel as it lasts far longer and is more efficient. It is also less likely to cling to the delicate petals and leaves after drying. Cornmeal and borax take longer to dry plant material. They may cling to petals and can be reused less often.

safety

Whenever you are using the microwave for drying make sure that you check the progress regularly and do not leave the oven unattended as overdrying is a fire risk and can occur very rapidly.

drying plant material using the microwave

1 POUR ABOUT AN INCH OF SILICA GEL INTO
THE BOTTOM OF A MICROWAVE-SAFE DISH.

2 TRIM ALL BUT ABOUT 2.5 CM (1 IN) FROM
THE STEM OF FLOWERS TO BE DRIED; HERBS
AND FOLIAGE CAN BE DRIED ON THE STEM.

3 POSITION THE STEMS IN THE SILICA GEL.

4 GENTLY SPOON SILICA GEL OVER THE
PLANT MATERIAL UNTIL IT IS COMPLETELY
COVERED

YOU WILL NEED

~

Silica gel

Microwave-safe dish

Florists scissors

Spoon

Small, soft paint brush

Wire cooling rack

Selection of plant material

safety

Cooking times will vary widely depending on a number of factors including the type of microwave, the type and quantity of plant material and any heat retained in the silica gel from previous drying cycles. Experimentation is vital though this must be watched at all times and flowers will need to rest and cool for at least 10 minutes before you attempt to remove them from the silica gel.

5 PLACE THE DISH IN THE MICROWAVE OVEN
– SEE PAGES 73 TO 75 FOR GUIDELINE
COOKING TIMES THOUGH YOU WILL NEED TO
EXPERIMENT YOURSELF.

6 REMOVE THE DISH FROM THE MICROWAVE
OVEN AND LEAVE FOR AT LEAST 10 MINUTES
BEFORE CAREFULLY POURING OFF SOME OF
THE SILICA GEL UNTIL THE PLANT
MATERIAL IS EXPOSED.

7 USING THE SMALL, SOFT PAINT BRUSH,
GENTLY BRUSH OFF AS MUCH OF THE SILICA
GEL AS YOU CAN WITHOUT DAMAGING THE
PLANT. LEAVE ON A WIRE COOLING RACK
AND BRUSH AGAIN BEFORE USING.

---

positioning plant material in silica gel

*Flowers – open-faced flowers like pansies and carnations
should be placed upright so that the flower head can be
filled with silica gel. Sprays such as statice and jasmine
should be laid horizontally

*Herbs – sprigs of herbs should be placed horizontally

*Foliage – foliage stems should be placed horizontally – if
leaves are flat you can stack two or three layers with silica
gel in a container each time

USING AND REUSING SILICA GEL

Silica gel is actually a crystal-like granule which can absorb up to 40 per cent
of its own weight in moisture and can be used time and time again. When
the granules are saturated with moisture they turn pink. It is then a simple
matter of spreading the silica gel out on a metal baking sheet and drying in
a conventional oven (about 250°F/103.3°C for 30 minutes should be
sufficient to return the granules to their original grey-blue colour). Silica
dust can irritate the nose and throat, so always use the gel in a well-
ventilated room. You may like to take the added precaution of wearing a
dust mask.

making stems

YOU WILL NEED

~

Toothpick or cocktail stick

Wire cutters

Floral tape

Fine gauge floral wire

Medium gauge floral wire

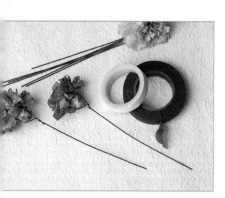

There is a variety of methods of extending the length of stem once you have dried the flower heads in the microwave oven, depending on the type of flower and the weight. All dried flowers are very fragile and need to be handled gently.

Carnations

Insert medium gauge wire into the flower head as shown, then bend down and twist to make a stem before covering in floral tape.

Strawflowers

These light flowers can be wired with a simple hook of medium gauge wire.

Roses

Simply extend the short length of woody stem with medium gauge wire bound with fine wire then taped.

Using Straw

Some flowers and grasses lend themselves to being extended with hollow straw stems, like this hydrangea flower, which is simply inserted into the hollow stem. You could use a spot of glue if you want to be sure of the stability of the join.

tip

Remember to keep the lengths in proportion with the original stems otherwise the flowers will look unnatural.

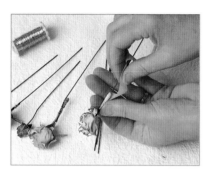
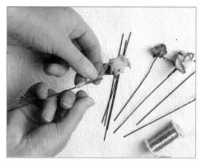

DRYING TIMES

Here are examples of drying times for some flowers, leaves and grasses based on using silica gel with an oven setting of around 280 watts (medium low in a 700 watt oven).

Remember never to leave the oven unattended, even if from experience you know the times are suitable for your oven and the quantity of material being dried.

FLOWERS	QUANTITY	BOX SIZE	SILICA GEL	TIME
Artemesia	4 stems	25 × 15 cm (10 × 6 in)	8 cm (3 in)	3 mins
Aster	5 asters 5 cm (2 in) diam.	25 × 15 cm (10 × 6 in)	8 cm (3 in)	4.5 mins
Gypsophila	2 stems	25 × 15 cm (10 × 6 in)	8 cm (3 in)	3 mins
Campion (Silene)	4 stems	25 × 15 cm (10 × 6 in)	8 cm (3 in)	3.5 mins
Candytuft (Iberis)	4 stems	25 × 15 cm (10 × 6 in)	8 cm (3 in)	3.5 mins
Carnation (Dianthus)	3 carnations 4 cm (1.5 in) diameter	10 × 10 cm (4 × 4 in)	8 cm (3 in)	3.5 mins
Chrysanthemum	3 button mums	10 × 10 cm (4 × 4 in)	8 cm (3 in)	5 mins
	8 mums	25 × 15 cm (10 × 6 in)	8 cm (3 in)	7.5 mins
Daisy	5 Gloriosa	25 × 15 cm (10 × 6 in)	8 cm (3 in)	3.5 mins
Globe Amaranth (Gomphrena globosa)	4 stems	10 × 10 cm (4 × 4 in)	10 cm (4 in)	4 mins
Goldenrod (Solidago)	4 stems	25 × 15 cm (10 × 6 in)	8 cm (3 in)	3.5 mins
Hydrangea	1 cluster	10 × 10 cm (4 × 4 in)	10 cm (4 in)	4 mins
Lady's Mantle (Alchemilla mollis)	2 stems	25 × 15 cm (10 × 6 in)	8 cm (3 in)	3.5 mins
Larkspur	4 stems	25 × 15 cm (10 × 6 in)	8 cm (3 in)	3.5 mins
Sea Lavender	4 stems	25 × 15 cm (10 × 6 in)	8 cm (3 in)	3.5 mins
Marigold	5 marigolds	10 × 10 cm (4 × 4 in)	8 cm (3 in)	3 mins

FLOWERS	QUANTITY	BOX SIZE	SILICA GEL	TIME
(Tagetes)	10 marigolds	25 × 15 cm (10 × 6 in)	8 cm (3 in)	6 mins
Sea Lavender	4 stems	25 × 15 cm (10 × 6 in)	8 cm (3 in)	3 mins
Pansy (Viola tricolor)	8 pansies	25 × 15 cm (10 × 6 in)	5 cm (2 in)	2.5 mins
Primrose (Primula)	1 large cluster	10 × 10 cm (4 × 4 in)	10 cm (4 in)	4 mins
Rhodanthe	4 stems	25 × 15 cm (10 × 6 in)	8 cm (3 in)	3.5 mins
Rose (Rosa)	6 roses (thin petals, not fully open)	25 × 15 cm (10 × 6 in)	10 cm (4 in)	5.5 mins
	rose buds	use open method		
	3 miniature roses	10 × 10 cm (4 × 4 in)	8 cm (3 in)	3.5 mins
Statice (Limonium)	5 stems	10 × 10 cm (4 × 4 in)	10 cm (4 in)	3 mins
Strawflower	3 flowers	10 × 10 cm (4 × 4 in)	8 cm (3 in)	3.5 mins
(Helichrysum bracteatum)	8 flowers	25 × 15 cm (10 × 6 in)	8 cm (3 in)	6 mins
Yarrow (Achillea)	3 stems	10 × 10 cm (4 × 4 in)	10 cm (4 in)	3.5 mins
Zinnia	3 flowers	25 × 15 cm (10 × 6 in)	8 cm (3 in)	4 mins
	5 flowers	25 × 15 cm (10 × 6 in)	8 cm (3 in)	5 mins

DRYING TIMES FOR LEAVES AND GRASSES

Because leaves are flat, you can stack two to three layers of leaves and silica gel in a box each time.

	QUANTITY	BOX SIZE	SILICA GEL	TIME
Lightweight leaves				
Maple	1 layer	25 × 15 cm (10 × 6 in)	2.5 cm (1 in)	3 mins
Strawberry	3 layers	25 × 15 cm (10 × 6 in)	8 cm (3 in)	7 mins
Sage				
Rose		25 × 15 cm (10 × 6 in)	10 cm (4 in)	5½ mins
Thicker leaves				
Camellia	1 layer	25 × 15 cm (10 × 6 in)	2.5 cm (1 in)	5.5 mins
Bay Laurel	3 layers	25 × 15 cm (10 × 6 in)	8 cm (3 in)	11 mins
Beech				
Eucalyptus	2 stems	25 × 15 cm (10 × 6 in)	8 cm (3 in)	10 mins
Ivy Trails	coiled 10–15 leaves	25 × 15 cm (10 × 6 in)	8 cm (3 in)	10 mins
Grasses eg				
Oats				
Wheat	4–6 stems	25 × 15 cm (10 × 6 in)	8 cm (3 in)	5 mins
Barley				

dried flowers

m o s s   p o l e

This decorative spiral of colour takes time to prepare.

YOU WILL NEED
~

Small clay flower pot

Plaster of Paris

Plastic bag

Short length of dried wooden stem
– we used dragon's claw willow

Everlastings

Dyed Phalaris grass

Lona

Dyed cluster-flowered
everlastings

Spagnum moss

Reel wire

Glue gun

Line the flower pot with the plastic bag then fill to around 5cm (2 in) short of the top with plaster of Paris. Set the piece of wood stem in the centre. Make a sausage of moss using the reel wire to hold it together. Once the plaster has set, wind the moss in a spiral around the post and fix in place. Using the glue gun, fix the flower and grass heads in a repeated pattern down the spiral. Finish off the bottom with more moss to cover the plaster.

tip

You could use dry flower foam instead of moss as the base though this will need some careful sculpting to fit well.

moss tree

Create your own instant bonsai with a combination of dyed moss
and dried flower heads for a permanent, easy-care tree.

tip

You could use fabric
or food dye to colour
the moss.

Line the flower pot with the plastic bag and fill up to within
5 cm (2 in) of the rim with plaster of Paris. Set the two long
stems and the shorter length in the plaster and leave to set.
Gradually build up the tree with pieces of moss, using the
glue gun to stick them to each other and the stem, until you
have the tree effect. Add heads of pot marigold randomly.
Cover the plaster of Paris at the base with green dyed moss
and add coloured Ti tree to the base.

YOU WILL NEED
~

Flower pot

Plaster of Paris

Plastic bag

Glue gun

Three lengths of dried wooden
stem – we used dragon's claw
willow

Dried and dyed Reindeer moss

Pot marigold (calendula
officianalis)

Ti tree

~PROJECT~

candlestick

Add an extra touch to a simple candlestick with a flower ring like this one. The natural browns and creams are a perfect complement to the golden brass.

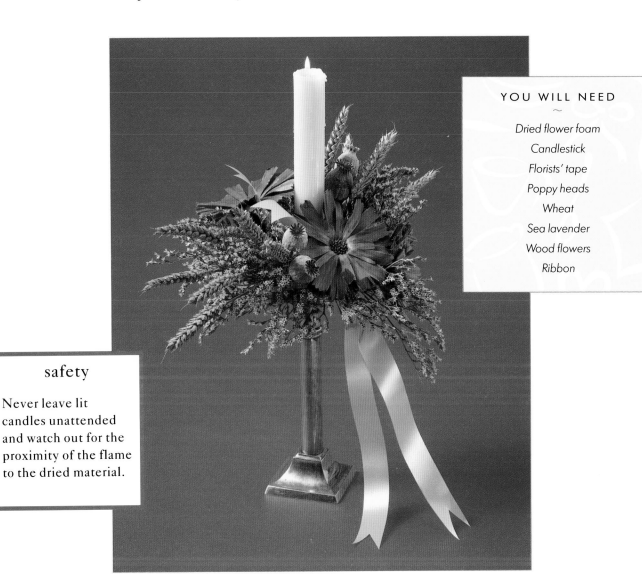

YOU WILL NEED
~

Dried flower foam
Candlestick
Florists' tape
Poppy heads
Wheat
Sea lavender
Wood flowers
Ribbon

safety

Never leave lit candles unattended and watch out for the proximity of the flame to the dried material.

Attach a block of foam to the base of the candlestick using tape. Start with the wheat ears, positioning them at the front and the back of the candlestick, then fill in and give more shape with the sea lavender. Add a couple of poppy heads, the wood flowers and ribbon to finish.

simple wreath

A perfect feature for a wall in place of a picture, this willow ring is punctuated with colour and texture.

YOU WILL NEED
~

Dyed Reindeer moss
Dyed yarrow
Mophead hydrangea
Ribbon
Willow ring
Glue gun

Using the glue gun, stick the moss, hydrangea and yarrow in clusters down both sides of the willow ring, then stick the ribbon to the back of the ring and hang.

~PROJECT~
hand tie

A free-standing splash of colour for side table or bookshelves, this hand tie is particularly effective with shades of yellow.

YOU WILL NEED
~

Deep yellow yarrow

Cluster-flowered everlastings

Sea lavender

Everlastings

Broom bloom

Protea

Stub wire

Ribbon

Scissors

Add wires to the flower heads so that they gradually reduce in length. Starting with the longest stems, build up the shape of the hand tie in your hand, adding a variety of stems all round. Because the stems are wired you will find it easy to slot extra colour in or change the balance until you are happy with the overall shape. Tie the bouquet tightly with a strip of ribbon then add the decorative bow. Trim the ends carefully until the bouquet is free-standing.

picture this

Make a feature of a favourite picture with a delicate posy and corner accents.

YOU WILL NEED
~

For the posy:
Dried flower foam
Safflowers (Carthamus)
Sea lavender

For the corner stem:
Coloured river grass
Brown glycerined beech
Stub wire
Fixing putty
Ribbon

tip

The sea lavender is a perfect foil for any coloured material you like to use.

Cut the floral foam into a neat, low block and cover with the sea lavender to make a posy shape. Add the safflowers for accents of colour. Bind short stems of beech and coloured grass together to make the corner details and stick these to the frame. Using the ribbon to link the picture and the posy, arrange the elements on the wall.

pure roses

Nothing beats the simplicity of rose buds used here in a vertical cluster in a rustic-style bark container.

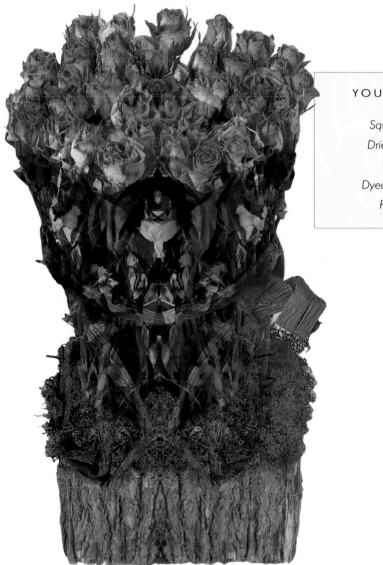

YOU WILL NEED
~

Square container
Dried flower foam
Dried roses
Dyed Reindeer moss
Paper ribbon

tip

Leave the stems as long as you can when drying, then add wire extensions which are hidden under the moss.

Cut the floral foam so that it fits snugly into the base of the container but sits about 2.5 cm (1 in) below the rim. Starting in the centre, arrange the roses in straight lines ensuring you don't crowd the flower heads. Continue adding stems until you are about 1 cm (½ in) from the edge of the container. Fill in the gaps with moss and finish with a ribbon tie.

blue jug

Extended heads of wheat and poppy make a silvery foil for the orange and blue features in this arrangement.

YOU WILL NEED
~

Jug

Dried flower foam

Protea

Wheat (Triticum)

Poppy heads

Dragon's claw willow

Wood flower

Everlastings (Xeranthemum)

Dyed Lady's Mantle (Alchemilla mollis)

tip

Collect poppy heads annually from the garden as they are always useful in arrangements.

Place the foam block so that it fits snugly in the jug and, starting with the longest stems first, add the foliage to the jug to make the basic shape. Add the protea and wood flower last to give the arrangement an accent and movement.

country posy

This hand-tied cluster of stems makes a lovely wall decoration in place of a picture, or make two to flank a favourite print on the wall.

YOU WILL NEED
~

Cluster-flowered everlastings

Wheat

Florists' wire

Ribbon

Pot marigold (Calendula officinalis)

Protea

Dried scrolls

Small quaking grass (Briza minima)

Group the stems in your hand, reducing the length gradually and securing occasionally with wire until the bunch is a suitable size. Try to keep the display quite flat as it will be hung on the wall. It may help to work with the back of the group on a table so that you only build up the front. Once complete, tie off firmly and finish with a coordinating bow.

table centre

A semi-permanent table centre such as this is a lovely way to dress the table up for even the simplest of meals. The pine cones give a festive feel and could be sprayed silver or gold to add a touch of glamour.

YOU WILL NEED
~

Small low container

Dried flower foam

Dyed Lady's Mantle (Alchemilla mollis)

Sea lavender

Pine cones

Dyed Ti tree

Candle

Florists' tape

Stub wire

Place the foam block in the base of the container. Fold stub wires to make pins and tape these around the base of the candle to hold it in place. Start with the sea lavender then gradually add the coloured stems to create the crescent shape before finally wiring the pine cones for the focal point below the candle.

picture swag

Even the plainest of pictures or mirrors can be made into a feature
with a simple cluster swag such as this.

YOU WILL NEED

~

Ribbon

Sea lavender

Dyed Reindeer moss

Dyed yarrow

Stub wire

Fixing putty

tip

You can use up lots of
odd flower heads in a
swag such as this.

The swag is built up by wiring together each of the elements in turn, using
the stems of the sea lavender to add to the length bit by bit. Continue
adding to the swag until it is the length you require, then simply drape or fix
in place with fixing putty.

victorian
pitcher

Large containers may be used when arranging microwave dried
materials, especially when they are combined with air-dried
materials to make a more interesting combination of textures.

YOU WILL NEED
~
Large jug
Dried flower foam
Poppy
Wheat
Dyed canary grass
Wood scrollings

Prepare the flower heads so you have varying lengths. The longest stems
need to be about 1½ times the height of the jug. Starting at the back,
gradually add to the overall shape of the arrangement. Add the purchased
wood scrollings for a focal point – you could spray these gold to give a more
dramatic finish.

~PROJECT~

decoy duck

The dyed grasses and natural deep yellows accentuate the colouring on this painted wooden duck and make an attractive focal point for a hall table or bedside.

YOU WILL NEED
~

Wooden duck

Dried flower foam

Glue

Golden yarrow

Sea lavender

Craspedia

Wild mignonette

Dyed reed canary grass

tip

If you don't want to glue the foam to the base permanently use a rubber solution formula that will peel off.

Mount a small oval block of foam on the back of the duck to give you enough material for the stems you plan to use. Start with the longer, slender stems then fill in the gaps with the sea lavender before adding the yarrow last of all, in the front.

country basket

A simple basket display such as this makes a perfect gift for many occasions. The easy-care decoration will be welcomed by many busy recipients.

> ## YOU WILL NEED
> ~
> *Basket*
> *Dried flower foam*
> *Lavender*
> *Wheat*
> *Protea compacta*

Cut the foam to fit the basket. Starting at the centre, put in a band of lavender before introducing the coloured wheat, then mix the two, taking the shape wide over the edge of the basket. Add the protea to the centre section to finish. Add an extra touch to the arrangement with a gift ribbon and cellophane wrapping.

FOOD
GIFTS

~ 6 ~

To use the microwave to cook food is, of course, the reason for its design and place in the kitchen. Owing to the way in which microwaves cook, the microwave oven is better suited for dealing with small quantities rather than batch-making, so you can make small amounts of preserves or sweets, ideal as a gift in a hurry. If you explore the full use of the microwave oven for food preparation there is a wide range of food gifts that you can make in your microwave. Additional inspiring presentation ideas will add that special touch. Sweet or savoury, there's bound to be an idea here that you can make your own with these inspirational but simple presentation ideas. For example, the small cross-stitch motif on the jam-pot covers takes just minutes to work. Melting chocolate in the microwave and using butter or ice-cube moulds to shape your very own handmade chocolates gives them a really personal touch.

safety

All the recipes are simple to follow, but remember the usual rules about microwave cooking and keep an eye on the cooking process, particularly as small quantities are being cooked each time and will quickly spoil if overheated. As cooking times may vary, check the instruction and recipe book for your particular oven for versions which have been tried and tested for your model. Recipes with a high sugar content need to be made in glass or pottery bowls as the high temperature reached by the sugar can damage plastic containers.

lemon curd

Add a touch of zest to your gift with these clever little jars of
lemon curd topped with salt-dough fruit slices.

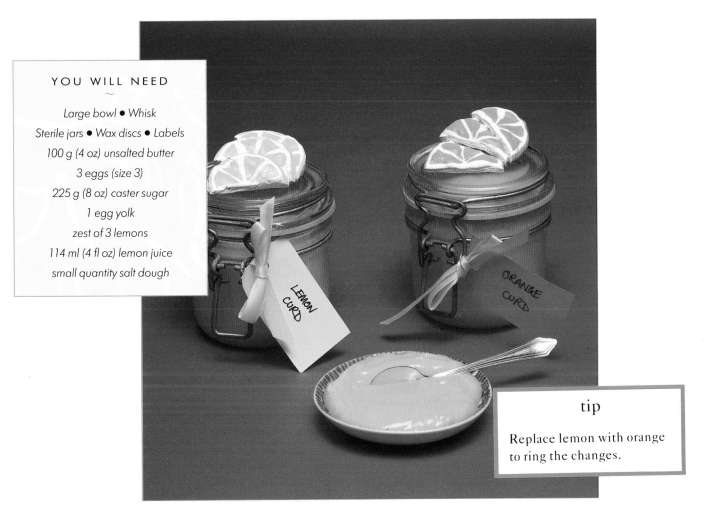

YOU WILL NEED
~

Large bowl • Whisk
Sterile jars • Wax discs • Labels
100 g (4 oz) unsalted butter
3 eggs (size 3)
225 g (8 oz) caster sugar
1 egg yolk
zest of 3 lemons
114 ml (4 fl oz) lemon juice
small quantity salt dough

tip

Replace lemon with orange
to ring the changes.

Melt the butter in a large bowl for 1 minute on full power. Whisk all the
other ingredients together then beat into the melted butter. Cook
uncovered on high for 2 minutes or until thick. Stir well and transfer into
sterile jars. Cover the tops with wax discs and seal. When cool, label.

Decoration

Make the fruit slices out of small quantities of salt dough (see page 13). Add
painted detail and seal with varnish before sticking on to the jar lids.

chutney

A traditional country recipe is perfect for this savoury treat. The plain jam jars are wrapped in hessian which makes an attractive alternative to a sticky label.

YOU WILL NEED
~

350 g (12 oz) skinned and chopped tomatoes

350 g (12 oz) cooking apple peeled, cored and chopped

1 medium onion chopped

225 g (8 oz) raisins

2 tsp salt

1 tsp ground ginger

1 tsp mustard

1 clove garlic crushed

225 g (8 oz) brown sugar

450 ml (¾ pt) malt vinegar

For the decoration:

Hessian fabric

Scissors

Raffia

Double-sided tape

Card label

Makes about 1.35 kg (3 lb) chutney.

Cook the tomatoes, apples and onions in a covered bowl on high for 8 minutes, stirring half way. Add the rest of the ingredients and mix well. Cook uncovered on high for 20 to 25 minutes, stirring from time to time. Allow to cool slightly before transferring to sterile jars and sealing. Decorate and label when cool.

Decoration

Cut a strip of hessian fabric long enough to fit around the jar with a small overlap. Fringe the edges. Wrap the fabric around the jar and tie a few strands of raffia in a bow to keep it in place. (You could use double-sided tape as well to stop the fabric from slipping around the jar.) For the lid, fix a strip of double-sided tape around the edge and remove backing paper. Place the lid in the centre of a piece of hessian 2 cm (¾ in) bigger than the lid all round. Press the fabric to the tape so that it forms a tight cover and trim the edges close to the lid. Add a card label.

truffle treat

Homemade chocolate truffles are an excellent gift for old and young – the handmade boxes make a firm container to stop them getting crushed.

YOU WILL NEED
~

125 g (3 oz) dark chocolate
15 g (½ oz) butter
1 egg yolk
Chocolate vermicelli

For the boxes:
Scissors
Thick coloured paper (or thin card)
Double-sided tape
Pencil
Ribbon

Break the chocolate into pieces and cook in a bowl on high for about 1 minute until melted. Beat in the butter and egg yolk then chill for about 1 hour. Shape the chilled chocolate mixture into small balls and coat with vermicelli. Pep the mixture up with a teaspoon of liqueur for a more luxurious offering.

To make the boxes:

Making the base – Cut a circle of thick coloured paper or thin card about 13 cm (5¼ in) in diameter. Then cut a strip of card or paper 8 cm (3 in) wide and long enough to fit around the circle with an overlap. Wrap the strip around the circle and fix the ends with double-sided tape. Push the circle up inside the card cylinder so that the base is recessed by about 1 cm (½ in). Use sticky tape to hold it in place. Recessing the base gives the box extra strength. Making the lid – Draw around the base on thick paper or thin card to make the circle for the lid for an accurate fit. Cut out and add a strip about 2 cm (¾ in) wide around the edge with an overlap as you did for the base. Fix with tape from the inside. Add ribbon decoration.

strawberry fair

Use small quantities of fruit to make your own jam. The pretty cross-stitch motif on the lid of the jar can be used time and again.

YOU WILL NEED
~

1 kg (2 lb) strawberries

675 g (1½ lb) sugar

Juice of one lemon

safety

Take care when handling the jam as the sugar makes the mixture very hot.

Makes 1.13 kg (2½ lb) of jam.

Using a glass or pottery bowl, cook the fruit and lemon juice on high for 7 minutes, stirring half way. Stir in the sugar and cook for a further 20 minutes on high, stirring from time to time. Look for gelling by chilling the syrup quickly, placing a small amount on an iced plate. Leave the jam to cool slightly before transferring it to sterile jars and sealing. Add labels and decoration when cool.

Cross-stitch motif

Cut a square of embroidery canvas approximately 6 cm (2½ in) larger all round than the lid of the jar. Pull out a few threads from about 1 cm (½ in) in from the edge to make a border. Work a strawberry motif in the centre of the square in cross-stitch using the pattern on page 110. Fix the fabric to the lid using double-sided tape around the edge, then add a fine bow to finish.

~ PROJECT ~

sweet shells

Melting small amounts of chocolate in the microwave is quick and simple and a shell-shaped butter mould makes the "handmade" chocolates look extra special.

YOU WILL NEED
~

Microwave-safe bowl
225 g (8 oz) chocolate

Makes about 16 shells.

Melt the chocolate in a bowl, cooking on high for about 1 minute. Mix well to ensure all lumps are melted then pour into moulds and leave to cool.

PRESENTATION

The chocolates are arranged in a purchased raffia basket with cellophane wrap and ribbon bows to decorate. You could add white and dark chocolate in separate layers to get two-tone chocolates or add both at the same time and stir with a cocktail stick for a marbled effect.

oaty cookies

These simple biscuits are quick to make and wrap in coloured corrugated paper, an ideal gift to take when visiting friends.

YOU WILL NEED
~

Cooking equipment
25 g (1 oz) wholemeal flour
25 g (1 oz) self-raising flour
50 g (2 oz) porridge oats
50 g (2 oz) soft brown sugar
½ tsp bicarbonate of soda
50 g (2 oz) soft butter
1 tbsp water to bind

For the wrapping:
Cellophane
Scissors
Coloured corrugated card
Double-sided tape
Ribbon

Makes about 12 cookies.

Mix all the ingredients together thoroughly to form a dough. Roll out on a lightly floured surface and cut into small rounds with a biscuit cutter. Arrange 6 to 8 evenly on the turntable and cook on high for about 3 minutes. Leave to rest for 1 minute before transferring to a cooling rack.

To wrap

Arrange the biscuits in two piles side by side on a sheet of cellophane or food wrap and seal. Cut a band of coloured corrugated card and wrap around the biscuit parcel, overlapping the ends and fixing with double-sided tape. Add a coloured ribbon to finish.

coconut ice

A traditional sweet recipe. The simple paper bags make this a
really charming gift for all.

YOU WILL NEED
~

Cooking equipment

Microwave-safe bowl

140 ml (¼ pt) of milk (use water
for crisper ice)

450 g (1 lb) caster sugar

125 g (5 oz) desiccated coconut

Pink food colouring

For the bags:

Scissors

Coloured paper

Glue

Double-sided tape

Box or book

Ribbon

Makes 450 g (1 lb) of coconut ice.

Using full power, heat the milk and sugar together in a large bowl, stirring
regularly until the sugar has completely dissolved. Cook for a further 6
minutes on high, checking and stirring every 2 minutes until the syrup
reaches the soft ball stage (test by dropping a small amount into cold water).
Stir in the coconut. Butter a shallow dish and spread half the mixture over
the bottom. Colour the remaining mixture and allow to cool slightly. Spread
over the top of the white ice. Chill in the fridge to set.

To make the bags

Cut a piece of coloured paper about 25 cm (10 in) long by 20 cm (8 in) deep.
Fold over one long edge 3 cm (1¼ in) and hold down with glue or double-
sided sticky tape. Wrap the paper around a small box or book with the
unfinished edge overhanging as it would if you were wrapping a parcel.
Neatly fold the raw edges in as if wrapping the box and stick in place.
Remove the box or book and you have an open-ended bag. Finish off by
making four holes in the top band for the ribbon closure and filling the bags
with coconut ice before tying closed. Make the basket in the same way
using a larger box or book as a mould and adding a paper band as a handle.

gingerbread

Little gingerbread figures are fun to make and this wrapping is
ever so simple.

tip

Make the holes for
the ribbons before
you cook the biscuits
if you want to hang
them up.

YOU WILL NEED
~
Cooking equipment
Microwave-safe bowl
50 g butter (2 oz) butter
75 g (3 oz) light muscovado sugar
2 tbsp honey
100 g (4 oz) wholemeal flour
75 g (3 oz) plain flour
2 tsp ginger
1 tsp bicarbonate of soda
1 small egg

For the wrapping:
Cellophane
Box or book
Card ● Ribbon ● Scissors

Makes about 16 small figures.

   Melt the butter, honey and sugar in a bowl on high for 1 minute, stir, a
further 1 minute and stir then a further 4 minutes. Sieve in flour and other
dry ingredients and mix to a dough. Add beaten egg to moisten if necessary.
Roll out on a lightly floured surface and cut with a biscuit cutter. Spread out
evenly on the turntable and cook on high for 2 minutes 30 seconds until dry.
Leave to stand for a minute before transferring to a cooling rack.

Presentation

Make a bag of clear cellophane by wrapping a strip around a box or book and
folding in one set of ends as if wrapping a parcel. Place a piece of card in the
bottom of the bag and fill with gingerbread shapes. Gather the top of the
bag and tie with ribbon.

popcorn special

Making popcorn in the microwave couldn't be simpler and these decorations are great for the kids to make as they can eat the leftover popcorn themselves!

YOU WILL NEED
~

Plain microwave popcorn (follow instructions on the packet)

or

2 tbsp of popping corn to 1 tbsp cooking oil

Lidded glass casserole

Colander

Kitchen paper

For the tree decorations:

Sewing thread

Gold or silver paint

Bows • Florists' wire

Ribbon

Place the oil and corn in the bottom of the casserole and stir so that all the corn is coated with oil. Setting the lid slightly askew so that some of the steam can escape, cook the corn on high for 5 minutes. Remove from the microwave and wait until the popping has stopped then turn the corn out into a colander lined with kitchen paper.

The next batch of corn will cook more quickly as the casserole will be hot from the previous batch so reduce cooking time slightly.

Tree decorations

Once the corn is cool, thread on to a length of double sewing thread and spray with gold or silver paint. Add tiny bows along the length of the garland. Alternatively, thread the corn on to florists' wire and bend into shape before spraying. Add a ribbon hanging loop.

f u d g e   a n d   n u t s

This is a fun way of decorating your front door – all the
components are edible. Each paper-wrapped square contains a
piece of homemade fudge.

YOU WILL NEED

~

Microwave-safe bowl

50 g (2 oz) butter

2 tbsp water

2 tbsp golden syrup

450 g (1 lb) granulated sugar

8 tbsp condensed milk

Mixed nuts

For the wreath:

Scissors

Thick card

*Coloured paper or sticky-backed
plastic*

Coloured foil

Ribbons

Double-sided tape

tip

Add chopped nuts,
cocoa powder or dried
fruit to the fudge for
extra flavour.

Makes 500 g (1 lb).

Cook the butter, water, syrup, sugar and milk together on high for 2
minutes, stirring at 1 minute, so that the sugar has completely dissolved.
Continue cooking the mixture for a further 5 to 6 minutes on high or until
the syrup mixture reaches the soft ball stage (test by dropping a small
amount into cold water). Beat the mixture until thick then pour into a
shallow dish greased with butter. Leave to cool, marking with squares
before it is totally set. Wrap the fudge squares in coloured foil and glue on
tiny ribbons. Fix the fudge parcels and nuts to the wreath using double-
sided tape. Tie a large bow and a hanging loop at the top to finish.

To make the wreath

Cut a circle of thick card about 20 cm (8 in) diameter, then cut a circle from
the centre to make the base for the wreath. Cover with coloured paper or
sticky-backed plastic to finish.

flavoured oil
and vinegar

A great treat for a culinary enthusiast, the oil and vinegar are
gently warmed to enhance the flavours.

YOU WILL NEED
~

For the oil:
Sunflower oil to fill container
Fresh herbs

For the vinegar:
White wine vinegar to fill container
Lemon

tip

If the bottle is too big
for the microwave or
features a metal
fastening like ours,
warm the oil in a
measuring jug with
the flavouring and
then transfer to the
bottle.

Wash and dry the herbs. Place a few sprigs in the bottle filled with oil and
warm gently on medium low for 5 minutes. Stopper and label.

Starting at the top of the lemon, cut a spiral of zest and place it in the
bottle. Add the vinegar then warm on medium low for 5 minutes. Stopper
and label.

Decoration

Cut strips of brightly coloured fabric with pinking shears and tie on to the
bottles. Add thin card labels.

~ P R O J E C T ~

f l a p j a c k s

These lovely chewy treats are great fun to make. The simply
wrapped boxes are decorated with a fan of paper.

Melt the sugar and butter in a glass or pottery bowl by cooking on high for
30 seconds. Stir in the syrup, salt, baking powder, oats, fruit and nuts and
mix well until it is all coated with the buttery mixture. Turn into a buttered
shallow dish and press lightly. Cook on high for 5 minutes then leave to rest
for 15 minutes before cutting into squares and placing on a cooling rack.

Decoration

Cover an empty chocolate box with wrapping paper and line the inside with
greaseproof paper. Fill with squares of flapjack. Pleat a long strip of
matching or coordinating paper into a fan and fix the ends together before
sticking to the top of the box with glue or double-sided tape.

peppermint creams

A perfect after-dinner treat to take with you. The chocolate
makes these peppermint creams a real luxury.

YOU WILL NEED
~

Microwave-safe bowl
1 egg white
275 g (10 oz) icing sugar
1 tsp peppermint essence
Green food colouring
100 g (4 oz) dark chocolate

Beat the egg white until light and frothy but not stiff. Add the sifted icing
sugar gradually until it forms a stiff dough. Add the green colouring and
knead. Roll out on a sugared surface and cut into shapes. Leave to set. Melt
the chocolate on high for 1 minute and stir well. Dip the peppermint creams
in the chocolate and place them on a cooling rack to set.

Presentation

Cover a long, narrow box with paper (we used an empty foil box cut down in
length). Line the inside with greaseproof paper or baking parchment. Fill
with sweets then use a ribbon to hold the box closed.

templates

All templates are shown at half size except Cross Stitch Pattern which is shown at actual size.

SIMPLE SHAPES

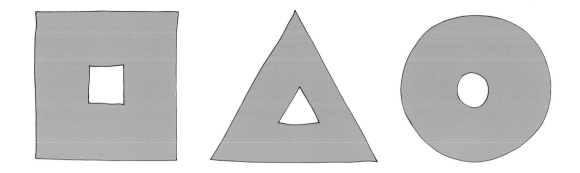

TREE TRINKETS

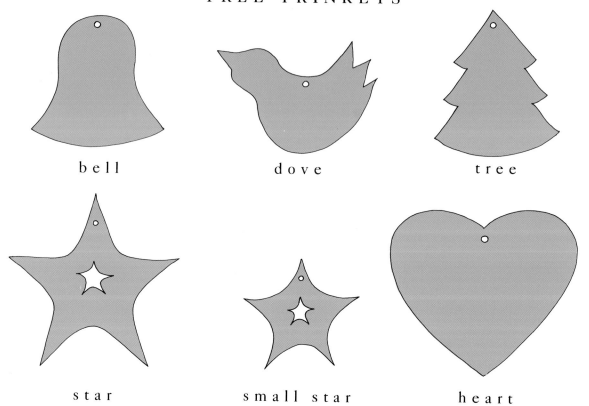

bell   dove   tree

star   small star   heart

~SALT DOUGH~
"TEA TIME"
salt dough fridge magnets

~SALT DOUGH~
VALENTINE HEARTS
Use heart template from Tree Trinkets as well.

~SALT DOUGH~
CELESTIAL INSPIRATION

~SALT DOUGH~
FLORAL FRAMES

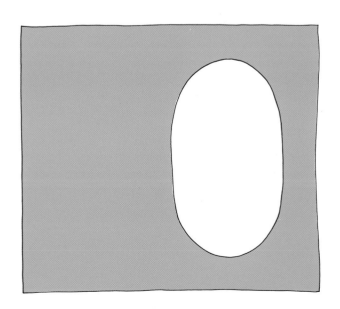

~SALT DOUGH~
ANIMAL MAGIC

giraffe

lion

bear

elephant

zebra

tiger

~TIE & DYE~
PRETTY POUCHES

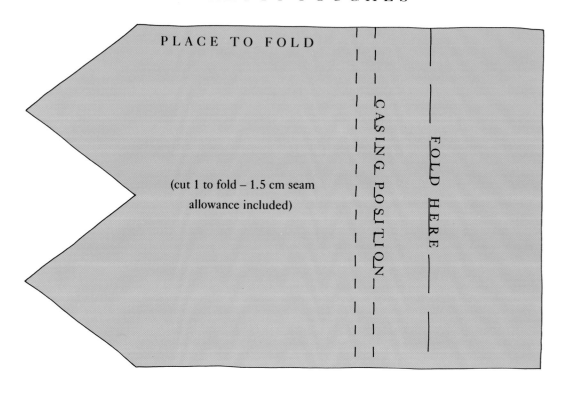

PLACE TO FOLD

CASING POSITION

FOLD HERE

(cut 1 to fold – 1.5 cm seam
allowance included)

~ PAPIER MÂCHÉ ~

SHAKER-STYLE BOXES: SET OF 3

LARGE BOX

BASE AND LID PATTERN
(dotted line is lid)

SIDE PATTERNS

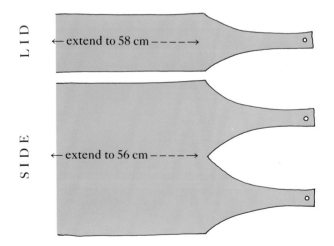

LID

←— extend to 58 cm – – – →

SIDE

←— extend to 56 cm – – – →

MEDIUM BOX

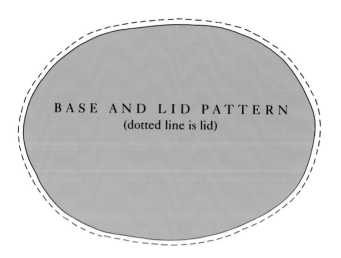

BASE AND LID PATTERN
(dotted line is lid)

SIDE PATTERNS

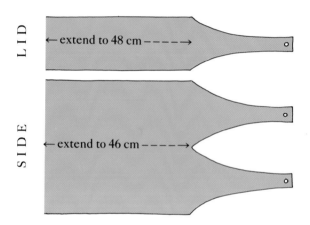

LID ← extend to 48 cm - - - - →

SIDE ← extend to 46 cm - - - - →

SMALL BOX

BASE AND LID PATTERN
(dotted line is lid)

SIDE PATTERNS

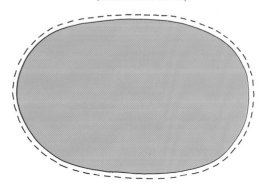

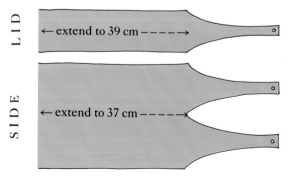

LID ← extend to 39 cm - - - - →

SIDE ← extend to 37 cm - - - - →

~PAPIER MÂCHÉ~
HAT PINS

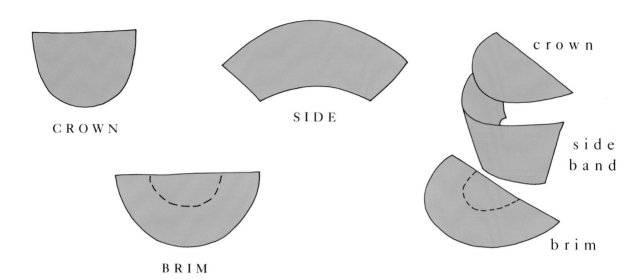

CROWN

SIDE

crown

side
band

BRIM

brim

~PAPIER MÂCHÉ~
JUGS

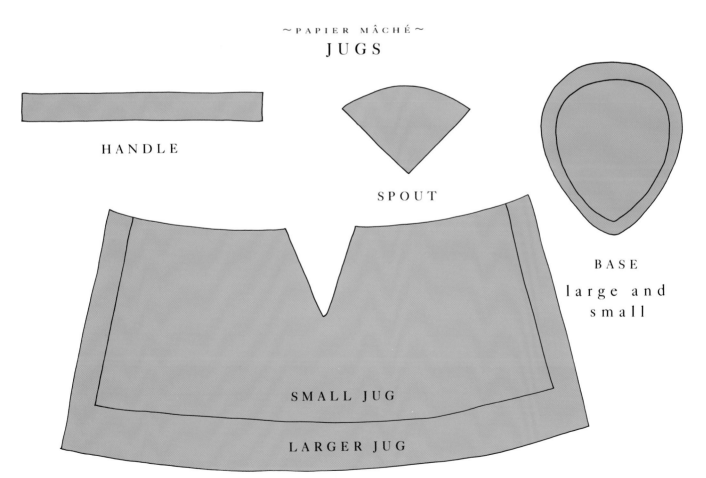

HANDLE

SPOUT

BASE
large and
small

SMALL JUG

LARGER JUG

~PAPIER MÂCHÉ~
HAPPY AND SAD MASKS

happy side · sad side

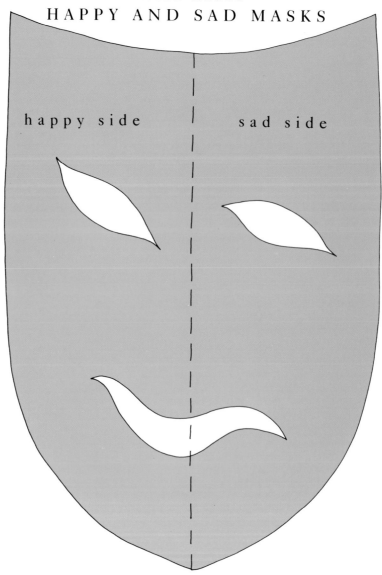

~FOOD GIFTS~
STRAWBERRY FAIR
CROSS STITCH PATTERN

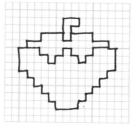

INDEX